AF843789

Clinician's Guide to SEXUALITY AND AUTISM

Clinician's Guide to SEXUALITY AND AUTISM

A Guide to Sex Education for Individuals with Autism Spectrum Disorders

JESSICA CAUCHI
Atlas Behaviour Consultation, Endicott College, Canada

PETER F. GERHARDT
The EPIC Programs, Endicott College, Canada

JUSTIN B. LEAF
Autism Partnership Foundation, Endicott College, United States

MARY JANE WEISS
Dean, Institute for Applied Behavioral Science, Endicott College, United States

ELSEVIER

ACADEMIC PRESS
An imprint of Elsevier

Academic Press is an imprint of Elsevier
125 London Wall, London EC2Y 5AS, United Kingdom
525 B Street, Suite 1650, San Diego, CA 92101, United States
50 Hampshire Street, 5th Floor, Cambridge, MA 02139, United States
The Boulevard, Langford Lane, Kidlington, Oxford OX5 1GB, United Kingdom

ISBN: 978-0-323-95743-4

For information on all Academic Press publications visit our website at https://www.elsevier.com/books-and-journals

Publisher: Nikki P. Levi
Acquisitions Editor: Joslyn T. Chaiprasert-Paguio
Editorial Project Manager: Barbara L. Makinster
Production Project Manager: Prasanna Kalyanaraman
Cover Designer: Miles Hitchen

Typeset by TNQ Technologies

Dedication

To individuals with autism and with other disability labels who have been denied access to, and acknowledgement of, their sexuality for far too long.

Contents

Appendix

Acknowledgments

The authors would like to thank Amy Gravino, Dr. Tracee Parker, and Dr. Thomas Zane for their insightful comments at various points in this process. They were all gracious with their time and talents and their efforts are greatly appreciated.

PART ONE

Introduction and foundational material

CHAPTER 1

Why is this book necessary?

Abstract

Sexuality education is of paramount importance for all, but especially for people on the Autism Spectrum. This book provides a comprehensive sexuality education curriculum for learners of all ages with autism. With an emphasis on assent and respect, this curriculum targets component skills across a variety of domains related to sex education. A review of evidence-based teaching strategies is also included, with reference to suggested methods for teaching throughout.

Keywords: ABA; Autism; Sex education; Sexuality.

For decades, sex education has been, and continues to be, perhaps the most controversial and complex instructional domain that (ideally) exists in educational curricula (Kendall, 2014). The reasons behind this controversy range from personal privacy to parent and/or student rights, community norms and personal biases, to religious beliefs and prohibitions. Beyond the controversy, human sexuality is complex in that it involves biology, psychology, personal preferences and idiosyncrasies, personal and familial values, sociocultural norms (Parchomiuk, 2022), and what may or may not constitute pleasure on an individual basis. To that end, the World Health Organization (2006) defines sexuality as being "experienced and expressed in thoughts, fantasies, desires, beliefs, attitudes, values, behaviors, practices, roles and relationships. [...] Sexuality is influenced by the interaction of biological, psychological, social, economic, political, cultural, legal, historical, religious and spiritual factors." (World Health Organization, 2006). In other words, human sexuality, and sex education, is complicated (e.g., Kendall, 2014).

At the same time, autism spectrum disorder (ASD) represents a complex expression of neurodivergence that is different for each person on the spectrum. The autism spectrum includes individuals with profound intellectual disabilities on one end and individuals with above-average intelligence on the other. It includes individuals with severely limited communication skills and social awareness to those with fluent language

Clinician's Guide to Sexuality and Autism
ISBN 978-0-323-95743-4
https://doi.org/10.1016/B978-0-323-95743-4.00007-2

and significant social awareness. And it includes individuals who display significant, potentially dangerous challenging behavior and those who do not. So, if we layer this diversity on top of the complexities of human sexuality, we get an extraordinarily complex multidimensional matrix of human behavior.

But everyone along the continuum of neurodiversity has the right to understand, to the greatest extent possible, their own sexual personhood; to express, to the greatest extent possible, their own sexual personhood; and to be safe, to the greatest extent possible, in their own sexual personhood. As such, comprehensive and individualized sex education tailored to the needs of autistic individuals should be considered an essential part of autism education (e.g., Bloor et al., 2022; Herrick & Datti, 2022).

Unfortunately, despite the importance of sex education, there is limited research documenting what constitutes effective sex education and/or intervention (e.g., Picard-Pageau & Morales, 2022) and for whom (e.g., Davies et al., 2021; McDaniels & Fleming, 2016; Stanojević et al., 2021). This is not entirely surprising given (1) the historical infantilization of people with developmental disabilities (Stevenson et al., 2011), societal discomfort with the topic of sexuality in general, let alone the sexuality of learners with autism (Herson et al., 1999), and (2) cultural disagreements as to the appropriateness of sex education provided outside of the nuclear family. For example, the Sexuality Education, and Information Council of the United States (SEICUS, 2021) noted sex education within a general education curriculum is a piecemeal collection of laws, ideologies, religious beliefs, and a mix of accurate and inaccurate information across states. They go on to report:

- Only **29** states and the District of Columbia mandate sex education.
- **35** states require schools to stress abstinence education.
- Just **16** states require instruction on condoms or contraception.
- **15** states do not require sex education to be any of the following: age-appropriate, medically accurate, culturally responsive, or evidence-based/evidence-informed.
- Only **9** states require sex education to include information on consent.
- Only **8** states require culturally responsive sex education.
- Just **7** states have policies that include affirming sexual orientation instruction on LGBQT identities or discussion of sexual health for LGBQT youth.
- **9** states explicitly require instruction that discriminates against LGBTQ people.

Source: *Sex Ed State Law and Policy Chart: SIECUS State Profiles 2021.* https://siecus.org/wp-content/uploads/2021/12/2021-Sex-Ed-State-Law-and-Policy-Chart-3.pdf.

This, in turn, results in an aspect of being human where there is high interest but little research, few programs, or even agreed-upon parameters for instruction/intervention.

The intent of sex education is to help individuals understand sexuality and sexual health, learn how to make safe decisions while decreasing rates of sexually transmitted diseases, and how to prevent sexual abuse (e.g., Schmidt et al., 2019). This, however, gets complex for autistic learners, given each individual's social, communication, and sensory profiles, which appear to "interact with access to information, motivation to engage in healthy sexual activities, and the development of skills needed to engage in healthy sexual behavior" (Solomon et al., 2019, p. 339). In addition, much of what constitutes the sex education provided to autistic learners is knowledge-based (e.g., completing quizzes or worksheets) instead of based in behavior skills training (BST) and dependent on the acquisition of the actual skills (e.g., Davies et al., 2021; Sala et al., 2019). In other words, successful outcomes are more often based on verbal responses to questions rather than on the display of an actual, relevant skill or skill set (Gerhardt et al., 2022) in the environment where it is most likely to be displayed. This is also troubling given that high verbal adults may know the language of sexuality, but this knowledge does not generally translate into the corresponding behavior (e.g., Kellaher, 2015).

Therefore, the necessity for this book that you now hold in your hand.

Sexual abuse, violence, and victimization

Sexual abuse, violence, and victimization generally refer to a broad range of perpetrator behavior including, but not limited to, rape, attempted rape, sexual assault, drug facilitated sexual assault, unwanted touching, incest, and sexual violation. What connects these topographies of criminal behavior is that all such acts are perpetrated in the absence of consent by the target/victim (Garvey & Senn, 2014). As such, a central goal of comprehensive sex education is the development of the skills associated with increased sexual safety (including personal advocacy and understanding boundaries) and a subsequent reduction in the prevalence of sexual victimization and violence (e.g., Schneider & Hirsch, 2020). Despite the importance of this goal, the majority of children, adolescents, and adults on the spectrum receive little, if any, in the way of such instruction (Barnard-Brak, et al., 2014). Further, Herrick and Datti (2022) suggest that since autistics generally receive limited sex education and are somewhat more likely than the general population to identify as a sexual minority (see Graham & Padilla, 2014), the need for comprehensive sex education may be even more critically important than it is for other groups.

Reported rates of sexual abuse and victimization of autistic adults are consistently higher than those reported by their neurotypical peers. Åker and Johnson (2020) reviewed the transcripts of actual police interviews with individuals with ASD and Intellectual Disability (ID) following allegations of sexual abuse in Norway. The authors reported that the majority of victims were female in their early twenties and were abused by someone they knew. Ohlsson Gotby et al. (2018) conducted a large (4500 individuals) population-based study in Sweden on the prevalence of the coercive sexual victimization or individuals with ASD and individuals with ADHD. The authors reported that women on the spectrum experienced a threefold increased risk of coercive sexual victimization while women with ADHD experienced a doubled risk. Most recently, Cazalis et al. (2022) reported the results of an online survey of 225 autistic women in France who were asked to complete an open question survey and a questionnaire derived from the Sexual Experiences Survey - Short Form Victimization. The results indicated that between 68.9% (open question survey) and 88.4% (sexual experiences survey) had experienced sexual violence, 66% of who reported being very young at the time of first assault. Multiple episodes of victimization were reported by 75% of the women.

Of particular relevance in Cazalis et al. (2022) is the author's argument that sexual victimization is more a function of personal vulnerability, than it is of being autistic (although autism acts as a vulnerability factor). This is important as it supports the importance of educating individuals on how to protect themselves more effectively from threats and acts of sexual violence; in other words, by being provided an evidence-based and comprehensive sex education.

Therefore, the necessity for this book that you now hold in your hand.

Sexual rights and pleasure

Sexual rights can be understood as including the freedoms, opportunities, and protections such that individuals or groups can engage in sexual expression, develop healthy sexualities, and have their sexualities accepted by the society in which they live (Tolman, 2006). Collectively, this can be understood as the right to access sexual pleasure (e.g., Alexander & Gomez, 2017). Calabrò et al. (2022) recently argued that autistic adults, just like the rest of the neurodiversity continuum, have the right to experience the best possible quality of life, including sexual well-being. The authors go on to argue that autistic adolescents and adults may require access to a sex coach which they define as "a trained professional who helps people with sexual, intimacy and relationship issues, [...] but also guides their clients to fully grasp their sexual potential through education, training, and communication" (p. 964). While this may be ideal, the continuing challenges to the simple provision of sex education make it difficult to imagine how this might become accepted practice in the near future.

Sexual pleasure, however, is about more than biology or physiology. Emotional context and relationships play a major role in feeling sexual pleasure or satisfaction. The sexual interest of adolescents and adults on the spectrum is comparable to that of neurologically typical adolescents and adults (e.g., Hancock et al., 2020) as is, to a somewhat lesser extent, the desire to be in a relationship. Dewinter et al. (2017) surveyed 675 autistic adolescents and adults and compared their reported sexual orientation and intimate relationship experience with general population peers ($n = 8064$). The results indicated that a majority of respondents with and without ASD, identified as congruent with their assigned gender at birth, have been attracted to someone of the opposite gender, and have been in at least one heterosexual intimate relationship. Autistic women reported a higher level of same-sex attraction and, and the same time, did not necessarily identify as female. About 50% of respondents with ASD reported being in a generally satisfying relationship and those in a relationship tended to live with their partner. Hancock et al. (2020) reported the results of a separate online study and noted that while the autistic adults who responded reported a similar level of interest in relationships to their general population peers, they also reported fewer opportunities to meet potential new partners and had shorter relationship duration. Importantly, they also reported learning less about sexuality from their peers.

Conclusion

At least in North America, sex education continues to be controversial and the sexual abuse and victimization of individuals on the spectrum, particularly females on the spectrum, remains unacceptably high (although, arguably, there is no acceptable level of abuse or victimization). While about 50% of high verbal adults reported being in a committed relationship, 50% did not, and we continue to know little about the sexual satisfaction of autistic adults either in isolation or in a relationship. More challenged individuals are, unfortunately, substantially absent the review literature. But for this group, there is more behavior analytic research on decreasing the "inappropriate" sexual behavior people on the spectrum (Mann & Travers, 2020), than there is on teaching appropriate, enjoyable, and safe sexual behavior in the form of masturbation (Cicero, 2019); problematic, but not exactly surprising.

As a society and as a field, we still have long way to go before evidence-based sex education is widely available and individuals with autism who want to be in romantic relationship can access the support they need, if they need it. We have a long way to go before the prevalence and associated trauma of sexual abuse and violence for individuals with, minimally, reduced. We have a long way to go before autistic individuals move from being marginalized members of society to just being members of society. We have a long way to go before more challenged autistic adults are seen, universally as true adults and no longer are infantilized when it comes to sexuality, independence, and participation in their own lives.

Basically, we have a long way to go. Therefore, the necessity for this book that you now hold in your hand.

CHAPTER 2
How to use this book

Abstract

This book is designed to be used with learners of all ages on the autism spectrum, with education provided by behavior analysts, teachers and educators, and parents. This chapter covers an outline of how to use the book to provide effective teaching in sexuality education with an emphasis on individualization for specific learners.

Keywords: ABA; Autism spectrum disorders; Caregiver; Clinician; Sex education; Sexuality.

When to start teaching sex education?

The short answer is as soon as possible! Most sexuality-related skills are complex and are comprised of myriad small, composite skills. Surprisingly, many of these composite skills are, on the surface, not related to sex at all. However, building strong foundational skills across the different domains will help lead to acquisition of the more complex skills related to sexuality.

Throughout the book, each skill has a suggested target age range listed. This is, as is everything else in this book, meant to be a guide. The age range listed alongside each skill is an indicator of when it may be appropriate to begin teaching the selected skill. Several skills should be targeted in the preschool/early school age years. It is possible that the individual you know is older than the suggested age range when you begin to use this book. In that case, you may need to go back and teach skills that were indicated for acquisition at a younger age. In other cases, you may not need to; use your best judgment about the appropriateness of skill and its priority in the individual's educational programming. Some skills simply do not apply to older learners; that is, one should ensure their 8-year-old learner has the preschool aged skill of saying no to unwanted physical contact, but would not need to ensure they can use preschool-appropriate slang for body parts.

In a broader sense, sex education should begin as early as possible. Sexuality is complex, and waiting until the skills are expected to be used is,

Clinician's Guide to Sexuality and Autism
ISBN 978-0-323-95743-4
https://doi.org/10.1016/B978-0-323-95743-4.00021-7

unfortunately, too late. Many skills will take a significant amount of time to teach, and it's important that they are mastered before they are expected to be used in everyday life. Including sex education as an early, and ongoing part of an education or treatment plan for someone with autism will help increase the likelihood that they will be safe, have an improved sense of well-being, and have an overall positive quality of life down the line. In addition, normalizing the discussion of these topics, as well as instruction in sexuality-related skills, helps to demystify these skills for instructors, autistic individuals, and family members. It is important to approach these skills as normal, appropriate, and essential. The earlier those messages can be sent, the earlier we are establishing the kind of positive, open environment that will help in the acquisition of these skills.

Who should teach these skills?

This book is designed for use by behavior analysts, teachers and other educators, parents, and anyone else involved in the consensual education of autistic individuals. Further considerations are warranted however. The first is the overall comfort level of the individual providing sex education. The person providing sex education should be knowledgeable in the topics presented, and comfortable discussing sexuality clearly, openly, and with direct language. When we are uncomfortable with the subject matter, we tend to be less direct, use more euphemisms and representative language, and "dance around" the topic. For learners on the autism spectrum, this makes understanding the facts of sexuality more complicated and more difficult. Ensuring that the instructor is presenting the information in a direct, clear, and neutral manner will help promote a much more positive educational outcome. Not all members of instructional teams will be comfortable in these roles; as with other elements of instruction, matching the instructor to the content area is an important element of successful teaching. In addition, we all have have limitations on our areas of instructional competence. As familar as many of us may be with masturbation or other physical aspects of sexuality, such familiarity does not translate into an ability to safely, effectively, or legally provide, say, hand over hand instruction in those areas.

The nature of some skills related to sexuality may make certain people in the learner's life more or less appropriate to function as the teacher/instructor. For example, it may be appropriate for a clinician in an ABA clinic to teach a 4-year-old child to label body parts, including penis, by using pictures, but it should be that child's parent or caregiver that teaches him to label that body part on himself. Conversely, when targeting slang for sexual acts, the learner's parents may not be the most knowledgeable or comfortable instructors.

A final consideration is the extent to which there may be unintentional lessons being taught alongside the intended lesson. For example, if multiple instructors are working with an individual in the bathroom to teach menstrual care the skill may be acquired, but so will, potentially, an understanding and/or acceptance that it is appropriate for different people to be in a private washroom with the student while she is performing a very personal and private skill. From a safety perspective, this is not something we would want the learner to be comfortable with; rather, we would like them to learn that unfamiliar adults should not be in private washrooms alone with you. There are many of these potential unintentional lessons within sex education, and careful consideration should be given to who is providing instruction, where instruction is provided, and how it is being provided. The team should consider these issues for each and every skill.

How to teach?

As will be reviewed in the next chapter, there are many evidence-based, behavior-analytic teaching strategies appropriate to teach skills to people with autism. Within each domain, the recommended teaching strategies are listed. These are cross-referenced with the strategies outlined in the following chapter and are provided as a recommendation only; consider them to be clinical suggestions. Overall, each skill should be broken down and taught to the learner in the way that best matches his or her individual learning profile.

In many cases, sex education will be provided to a learner as a part of a more comprehensive overall program of instruction. The clinician, educator, or caregiver likely already knows effective teaching strategies for a particular individual learner. The target skills within this book should be taught using evidence-based strategies that best apply to that individual learner. In many cases several teaching strategies are listed for the same skill domain. In these cases, all teaching strategies may be appropriate and the instructor should choose the one they think will be most effective based on what they already know about the learner. It may be that the same instructor teaches one skill to a particular learner using one teaching strategy and the same skill to another learner using a different strategy. In other words, interpret the information as guidelines and suggestions based upon your knowledge and history with the learner in question.

Consent and assent

Perhaps more so than in any other instructional domain, both parent/guardian consent and student assent needs to be obtained prior to instruction being provided. Parameters of instruction including specific goals, teaching methodology, and potential benefits and risk need to be explained to both the parent guardian and the individual learner. In addition, aspects such as who will be providing instruction, how often instruction is to take place, where it is to place, and how acquisition will be measured need to be fully disclosed in advance of teaching. Barriers and limits to confidentiality should be delineated as well, to help ensure everyone is comfortable with their particular roles in the process.

In terms of assent, both verbal and behavioral indicators of student assent should be identified prior to the onset of instruction. In addition, the student needs to be free to terminate instruction should they desire. This does not necessarily mean that instruction completely stops. Rather, it indicates that, perhaps, a reevaluation of how instruction is provided is necessitated. Overall, recognizing that sex education can be a deeply personal, value-heavy, and sometimes uncomfortable topic means that ongoing assent to teaching should be emphasized.

One way to think about sexual behavior is to think about it as, well, behavior. The skills included here in sex education are all overt or covert behavior, meaning they can be taught the same way that other skills are taught to individuals with autism. The same behavior analytic principles of reinforcement, prompting, social validity, generalization and maintenance all apply. This can help make the inherent instructional challenges seem a bit less formidable.

Finally, the skill sets focused on within sexuality instruction are broad, multifaceted, chained, and context-specific. While the skills listed are considered component skills, as in, they are smaller components of broader composite skills, they will likely still need to be broken down into smaller parts to teach. The ways in which skills can be chained together is individualized and, often, nuanced. Contextual factors can change everything about identifying the best behavioral option in a situation; hence, the individualization of strategies is the most important message. As in all other behavioral intervention approaches, it is important for us to assess the needs and tailor intervention for the individual in a highly specific, individualized manner.

Where should sex education be taught?

This will vary by learner. In general, teaching should only occur in a classroom or larger group setting once the learner has demonstrated ability to learn effectively in that type of setting. For some individuals, group instruction may be difficult and 1:1 teaching may be required. Conversely, many of the social interaction type skills will be more difficult to teach without peers to practice with. As such, some of the more overt social skills may be more appropriate for group instruction. Additionally, while some skills are objective (e.g., body parts), others may be more personal (e.g., preference in sexual acts), and may be more appropriate to target in a less shared setting.

Who should receive sex education?

Everyone! While this book is intended to provide a comprehensive overview, some skills will be more or less relevant to individual learners. Adaptations can be made for nonvocal communicators, those that use alternative forms of communication, and those with lower levels of independence in self-care. It should not be assumed that there is anything about an individual's diagnosis, level of communication, current social interactions, cognitive functioning, or academic performance can tell us anything about their interest in sex. The skills contained in this book are important for helping ensure an individual's safety, independence, and quality of life related to sex.

The use of peers

Throughout the various instructional domains in this book. special consideration is given to the use of peers as a resource. As "with it" or well-informed any practitioner may consider themselves, they are most definitely missing information about the kind of slang teens use, what sort of apps school-age kids are using, and how preteens talk about sex, and how teens are accessing pornography. The only accurate point of reference for this information is the community in which the learner belongs. Same age peers, people in their school, and other community members will provide valuable information as to how to modify instructional targets, what should be the most "current" goal, and how to prioritize instruction. However, the issues of risk can never be separated from goal development or the selection of instructional methods; safety and risk must be embedded into every instructional decision.

Values and preference

There is arguably no area more tied to individual preference than sexuality. People are attracted to the gender to which they are attracted, like different sexual positions, are attracted to different physical characteristics, and they swear by different brands of tampons. Simply put, people are individuals. Individual preference needs to be considered and respected within all aspects of sexuality education. This may be even more true for individuals with disabilities given their recognized limited access to information. Sadly, the recognition of sexual needs, desires, pleasures, and preferences of autistic individuals has been delayed, if not ignored entirely. As such, our attention to this is overdue and an essential element of service provision.

Values are equally important to acknowledge. All individuals have values and biases, including the learner, their family and community, and the instructors themselves. Working within the family unit to recognize and be respectful of values, while at the same time teaching fact-based education is challenging. Clear identification of everyone's roles in the teaching and goal selection process from the outset may help prevent future difficulty.

Instructors will also be approaching sex education with their own biases and values. Instructors need to be aware of this and remain as neutral and fact-based as possible. Occasionally, situations may arise where the values of the learner, their family, or the instructor are too different from the values of the instructor and this can be problematic. In these situations, it may be best to refer the provision of sex education to someone else whose values may be more compatible with those of the individual or their family. This may not be discussed as the discussion can be uncomfortable. However, the effective management of these issues helps to ensure that instruction continues, that these goals remain in focus, and that the individual with autism's needs remain paramount.

Other resources

Many additional resources are provided at the end of this book. This book is meant to help instructors know what to teach within sex education, but is not meant to be a resource about sexuality in and of itself. Resources related to content are included, and practitioners are recommended to familiarize themselves with the related content prior to teaching.

Additionally, the scope of this book was narrowed to only skills related to sexuality education. There are many domains included here where broader education is likely to be of benefit to the learner (e.g., social skills, health, and hygiene). The skills recommended here are only those that directly pertain to sexuality.

Final considerations

Use real, direct, and clear language when teaching. Avoid innuendo and euphemism. Likewise, real materials and realistic visuals should be used wherever possible.

Consider independence as a spectrum rather than a binary measure. While the best outcome may be for an individual to tolerate wearing sanitary pads, recognize when they need to be changed, monitor their cycle, and manage all needed materials; some learners may not attain this level of mastery. It is suggested that teaching the individual to use period underwear independently is preferential to requiring support to complete all of the above skills from a paraprofessional. Likewise, a nonvocal communicator may be taught to take photos on their phone of relevant events in their day to share with a caregiver, instead of presuming they are unable to recall and talk about their events. Creativity in programming and a broad definition of independence will be important to ensure each learner reaches their maximum potential.

Defining transfer to the natural environment as the end goal. A limitation associated with teaching sexuality skills to autistic learners is transferring individual skills to real-life environments. For example, learning to put on a condom effectively and independently in practice alone in one's room is much different than doing so in a sexual situation with a partner when one's body is full of hormones, adrenaline, and overall excitement. Simply put, just because the individual has been taught the skill doesn't mean they will be able to use it when they need it. Practicing in as close to real-life as possible may help. Mastery criteria for safety skills and those with high risk (e.g., proper use of menstrual materials, proper use of birth control) should have stringent mastery criteria, while skills that are more social in nature should be taught to a level of mastery that is common for other peers in their setting (e.g., most of us stumble on first dates!).

Be flexible in instruction. Finally, sexuality and all its components are some of the most complex aspects of human life. While teaching in this area, especially for those on the autism spectrum, is so incredibly important, it is also challenging. Skills may require multiple attempts to find the best way to teach, and many skills should be reassessed and retaught as learners grow and develop and mature. Instructors maintaining some patience, creativity, and sense of humor will go a long way to making this a comfortable situation for their learner.

CHAPTER 3
Interventions

Abstract

When teaching about sexuality to people, it is extremely important to utilize evidence-based teaching strategies. This chapter will review several evidence-based teaching strategies used commonly within the field of ABA including Behavioral Skills Training, Teaching Interaction Procedure, Cool vs. Not Cool, Video Modeling, and others. It is important to individualize teaching per the individual in all cases, and by providing an overview in this manner it is our hope that the clinician will be able to create a teaching plan that is evidence-based and well suited for the individual learner.

Keywords: ABA; Autism; Behavioral skills training; Discrete trial teaching; Evidence-based practice; Learner; Parent coaching; Practitioner; Sex education; Video modeling.

As this book reflects, sex education is of the upmost importance for individuals diagnosed with autism spectrum disorder (ASD). Teaching the concepts of sex, sexual health, and dating should occur as early as the learner is ready for such instruction. These skills are often difficult to teach and require the learner to make fine discriminations. For example, when teaching a learner how to ask someone out on a date, they will have to pay a great deal of attention to behavioral indicators of whether the other person is interested in going on a date with them. Further, a learner might also have to discriminate where to display certain skills and where not to display certain skills. For example, if we were teaching a client about masturbation we would want to teach them that they should engage in this behavior in the privacy of their own room or home (if it is not a shared space) as opposed to masturbating in public.

These discriminations are important to make because if the learner makes an incorrect discrimination there may be serious negative consequences. For example, in the previous examples, if a learner fails to recognize the signs that a person is not interested in dating them, this can result in everything from being ridiculed to involvement with the criminal justice system. In the second example, if a learner fails to correctly discriminate when to masturbate it can mean the difference of self-pleasure

Clinician's Guide to Sexuality and Autism
ISBN 978-0-323-95743-4
https://doi.org/10.1016/B978-0-323-95743-4.00002-3

versus arrest for indecent exposure. Professionally we are ethically required to implement procedures that are effective, evidence-based (APA Presidential Task Force on Evidence-Based Practice, 2006), and empirically supported (LaRoche & Christopher, 2009). If we fail to implement procedures that meet these criteria we may be inadvertently causing harm to our learners.

In 2017, DiGennaro-Reed et al. defined evidence-based practice as: "the process of using results from high-quality research to inform clinical practice, while also taking into consideration clinical experience and expertize, and the individual characteristics, culture, and preferences of a client (p. 142)." Within this definition, it is critical that a practitioner takes into consideration the preferences of the client and/or the caregivers. If a client and/or the caregivers prefer a procedure, as long as it is a proven effective procedure, it would be wise for the practitioner to implement that procedure. If, however, a client and/or the caregivers prefer a procedure for which there is no evidence of effectiveness, the practitioner should not be implementing that procedure, as it could cause harm to the learner. Instead, the practitioner should discuss with the client and/or caregiver why implementing that procedure is not in their best interest and offer alternative solutions.

In the most recent version of the Ethics Code for Behavior Analysts Certification Board (2020), the (second) Core Principle, Treating Others with Compassion, Dignity, and Respect, emphasizes the importance of personal choice in care, and also discusses the importance of ensuring that clients have knowledge to make informed choices. Furthermore, the Code now explicitly highlights and values self-determination. As such, practitioners need to focus on collaboration with clients, and on empowering them to chart, to whatever extent possible, their own course. Navigating the commitment to empowering clients along with the commitment to evidence-based practice can be challenging. However, these values are neither incompatible nor negotiable.

The second consideration is that practitioners should only implement procedures for which they are trained, and which falls under their scope of competence (Behavior Analysts Certification Board, 2020). For example, if a practitioner is trained in implementing video modeling but not trained in the teaching interaction procedure, then they should be implementing video modeling. If, however, the learner requires a procedure for which they are not trained in (e.g., the teaching interaction procedure) then the practitioner should refer the learner to a professional who can provide the needed intervention with a high degree of quality and fidelity, or the practitioner should seek out additional training or mentorship. These guidelines exist to ensure that clients are not subjected to inferior care, and to ensure that intervention provided is always in the best interests of the client.

Finally, a practitioner must adhere to the empirical evidence for any given procedure. When evaluating the research on a procedure, the practitioner first should determine if the procedures are effective, or if there could be some other explanations to why behavior change occurred (e.g., other procedures were also provided). For example, there has been a plethora of research on Social Stories (Backman & Pilebro, 1999; Chapman & Trowbridge, 2000; Rowe, 1999). However, when closely examining the research, in most studies evaluating Social Stories, they are usually implemented concurrently with other behavior modification procedures that may be the more likely reason for behavior change (Reynhout & Carter, 2006; Test et al., 2011). Second, a practitioner should also determine if the procedures are well defined within the research, so that the practitioner can either replicate or partially replicate them in clinical practice. Further, the practitioner should evaluate if the researchers implemented the procedures to a high degree of fidelity. Third, the practitioner should evaluate if there is a functional relationship between the procedure and the change of behavior. Fourth, the practitioner should analyse if the results did not only result in a change in behavior but if that change was meaningful. Finally, the practitioner should conduct a deep dive to identify if the results have been replicated across different studies and research labs (Horner et al., 2005). If a procedure meets all of these criteria, then a practitioner should feel confident in implementing that procedure. If a procedure does not meet these criteria, the practitioner should avoid the procedure.

Today, there are myriad interventions out there for individuals diagnosed with ASD (e.g., social thinking or the Circles (tm) curriculum), many of which would be considered fad treatments (e.g., Addison et al., 2012; Chambless et al., 2001; Esch & Carr, 2004; Jacobson et al., 1995; Jacobson et al., 2015; Jacobsonb & Mulick, 1994; Matson et al., 2013; Mostert, 2001). Some of these fad treatments may just be a waste of time or money for the families; other fad treatments can cause serious negative harm for the learner. As such, when teaching sexual education, it is imperative for the practitioner to avoid fad treatments. Fortunately, there are many interventions that have been found to be effective, that are evidence-based, and that are empirically supported for individuals diagnosed with ASD. Further, there are numerous interventions that are conceptually systematic with behavior analysis. In this chapter we will provide the reader with a description of different interventions that can be implemented and suggestions on how they could be implemented. It should be noted that this is not a comprehensive list; it is a description of those procedures that we have found to be some of the most effective within our research and clinical practice.

The interventions

Discrete trial teaching

One of the most common procedures in the field of behavior analysis is discrete trial teaching (DTT; Lovaas, 1981, 1987). Discrete trial teaching is a systematic teaching procedure that breaks skills down into smaller components and teaches these steps one at a time. Discrete trial teaching consists of the practitioner implementing a series of teaching trials within a given session. These teaching trials consist of three mandatory components. First, the practitioner provides an instruction/discriminative stimulus (e.g., "Name a person who is your friend"). Next, the learner responds to that instruction (e.g., saying "Kenny"). Finally, the practitioner provides a consequence based upon the learner's response. If the learner responds correctly, then the practitioner would provide reinforcement (e.g., a toy, token, social praise). If the learner responds incorrectly, then the practitioner would provide feedback (e.g., saying "no," removing a token, providing the correct answer).

Often, the learners we work with have difficulty in responding correctly and, therefore, the practitioner might need to prompt the learner to respond correctly. Thus, the fourth optional step of discrete trial teaching is the provision of a prompt. When the practitioner provides a prompt, they should do so following the instruction but prior to the learner's response. There are numerous ways a practitioner can provide a prompt (e.g., verbal, gestural, multiple alternatives, physical, etc ...). A practitioner should not be providing or fading prompts without a system in place. Prompting systems are guidelines of when a learner should provide a prompt and when an instructor should fade a prompt (Cengher. et al., 2018; MacDuff et al., 2001). There are many different prompting systems that are used for individuals diagnosed with ASD today. These include most-to-least prompting (Fentress & Lerman, 2012; Longino et al., 2022), least-to-most prompting (Libby et al., 2008), constant time delay (Miller & Test, 1989), progressive time delay (Walker, 2008), simultaneous prompting (Waugh et al., 2011), and no-no prompt (Leaf et al., 2010). While research has shown that these prompting systems are effective, they can be administered in a very rigid manner. Ideally, prompts should be individualized and applied in flexible ways.

As such, we would recommend practitioners use flexible prompt fading when implementing discrete trial teaching (or any procedure for that matter). When a practitioner uses flexible prompt fading, they make in-the-moment decisions about if they should prompt, if they should not prompt, and what prompt type to use (Leaf, Leaf, Alcalay, et al., 2016). Thus, with this system a practitioner can use any of the prompt types at any time as they see fit. However, this is not based upon a gut feeling or done randomly, but rather following certain guidelines. First, the goal of the practitioner should be to keep the learner responding correctly (prompted or unprompted) at 80% accuracy within a teaching session. Second, when a practitioner decides to prompt, they should provide a prompt that they have deemed will likely result in a correct response but that is the least assistive as possible. Third, the goal should be that the practitioner reduces the provision of prompts as quickly as possible. During each trial, the practitioner should ask themselves if they believe the learner is going to respond correctly. If the answer to that question is yes, then the practitioner would not provide a prompt. If the answer to that question is no, then the practitioner should decide what is the least assistive prompt necessary to elicit a correct response. This should occur during every teaching trial. The reason for the preference for flexible prompting is because it promotes independence and guards against dependency on cues from the instructor.

Although discrete trial teaching is often associated with younger learners or learners with more impacted cognition, the reality is it can and should be used with learners of all types (Smith, 2001). It is a great approach as it is systematic, breaks the skills down, and provides the learners with multiple opportunities to learn the targeted skill. Research and clinical practice have demonstrated that DTT can be effective in teaching conversation skills (e.g., Ingvarsson & Hollobaugh, 2010), play and social skills (e.g., Nuzzolo-Gomez et al., 2002; Shillingsburg et al., 2014), and language skills (e.g., Conallen & Reed, 2016; DiGennaro-Reed, Reed, Baez, & Maguire, 2011). It is also a procedure that can teach a variety of skills in regard to sexual education. For example, it could be utilized to teach the learner to discriminate among different relationships, how to talk to people they are interested in dating, how to buy different sexual prevention and/or sex toys, and to discriminate healthy and unhealthy sexual relationships and behavior. Discrete trial teaching is often used to teach conditional discriminations (Kodak & Grow, 2011), and thus could be used to teach skills in areas related to how to determine if consent is or is not being given, determinations regarding the appropriateness of online behavior, and even whether a pad should be changed.

Cool versus Not Cool

Another procedure that can be used to teach sexual education is the Cool versus Not Cool (tm) Procedure (Leaf et al., 2012). The Cool versus Not Cool Procedure is a social discrimination procedure that is empirically evaluated and has been found to be effective to teach a variety of skills to autistic/individuals diagnosed with ASD (Ferguson et al., 2021; Leaf, Leaf, Milne, et al., 2016; Milne et al., 2017). The purpose of this teaching procedure is to help the learner discriminate what behaviors are socially appropriate (e.g., "Cool") and what procedures are socially inappropriate (e.g., "Not Cool") and, ultimately, display the appropriate behavior in their natural environment.

The procedure starts with the practitioner stating what skill they are going to be working on during the teaching session (e.g., the practitioner saying "Today, we are going to be working on how to talk to someone you might be interested in"). Next, the practitioner instructs the learner who they should be paying attention to (e.g., the practitioner saying "I want you to pay attention to me as I start a conversation with someone I think is interesting"). Then, the practitioner provides a cue that they are about to act out the scene (e.g., the practitioner saying "ready set action"). Next, the practitioner demonstrates the behavior either the socially appropriate way (e.g., approaching the person and asking some socially acceptable question) or an inappropriate social way (e.g., checking out the person explicitly for a long duration or asking an overly personal question such as, "What is your address?" Following the demonstration, the practitioner provides a cue that the demonstration is over (e.g., the practitioner saying "cut") and asks the learner if the demonstration was either "cool" or "not cool." If the learner responds correctly, the practitioner provides reinforcement (e.g., praise or a token). If the learner responds incorrectly, the practitioner provides corrective feedback. Next, the practitioner asks the learner why the demonstration was "cool" or "not cool." If the learner responds correctly, the practitioner provides reinforcement (e.g., praise or a token). If the learner responds incorrectly, the practitioner provides corrective feedback. The practitioner then can implement further demonstrations if needed.

An optional component of the cool versus not cool procedure is having the learner role-play the targeted behavior. During the role-play component the practitioner should set up situations for the learner to engage in the targeted behavior. The goal of the role-play should be that the learner is going to practice the behavior the appropriate way. The practitioner starts off by providing a cue to the learner to start the role-play (e.g., saying "ready set action"). The learner then role-plays the behavior. Following the role-play, the practitioner provides a cue that the demonstration is over (e.g., the practitioner saying "cut") and asks the learner if they role played the behavior either "cool" or "not cool." If the learner responds correctly, the practitioner provides reinforcement (e.g., praise or a token). If the learner responds incorrectly, the practitioner provides corrective feedback. Next, the practitioner asks the learner why the role-play was "cool" or "not cool". If the learner responds correctly, the practitioner provides reinforcement (e.g., praise or a token). If the learner responds incorrectly, the practitioner provides corrective feedback. The practitioner then can implement further demonstrations if needed.

There are several important guidelines that a practitioner should follow throughout the implementation of the Cool versus Not Cool Procedure. First, it is considered important, when appropriate, for the practitioner to model the behavior both the appropriate way and the inappropriate way. It is important to model the correct way so that the learner knows what behavior they should be displaying. It is, however, also important for the practitioner to demonstrate the skill the inappropriate way because many of the skills may be nuanced and the practitioner must highlight what steps are being missed or omitted. This helps with the discrimination of appropriate versus inappropriate behavior in the particular context. Second, generally speaking, although we want the practitioner to demonstrate both the appropriate and inappropriate behavior, we want the learner only to model the appropriate behavior. This way, the learner is practicing displaying the behavior correctly and the practitioner can reinforce that behavior. Third, when the practitioner models the behavior the incorrect way, they need to display the behavior the way the learner is usually displaying the behavior in the natural environment (e.g., getting steps incorrectly or omitting certain behaviors). This way, it highlights to the learner exactly what they are not doing in the natural environment. Fourth, both in the demonstration and modeling components of the Cool versus Not Cool Procedure there should be multiple exemplars; meaning that there should be different situations being used. This consideration is important because using multiple exemplars can help increase the learner with generalizing their behavior to the natural environment. Fifth, there does not need to be an equivalent number of "cool" and "not cool" demonstrations. Rather, the practitioner should decide if it is important to demonstrate more cool behaviors or not cool behaviors. If the learner would benefit from seeing the behavior demonstrated correctly then the practitioner would provide more cool demonstrations. Conversely, if the learner is missing components of the behavior or omitting important aspect of the behavior the practitioner might elect to have more not cool demonstrations. Generally speaking, there will be many demonstrations of cool behavior, to assist with strengthening this aspect of skill development. Sixth, the practitioner does not need to use the words "cool" or "not cool"; the practitioner can use whatever language is appropriate to the learner's culture and geographic location. Finally, it is important for the practitioner to be aware that this procedure may result in the learner displaying emotional responding. This is because the learner may be sensitive to working on sexual behaviors, and because the procedure implies the identification of past or current missteps. Clinicians should frame this proactive positively, ensure that all practice is done with compassion and sensitivity, and should adjust instruction to ensure comfort.

The Cool versus Not Cool Procedure started out as a clinical procedure used to teach a variety of social behaviors to autistic/individuals diagnosed with ASD. However, in the past 10 years, research has been conducted on the effectiveness of the Cool versus Not Cool Procedure (Ferguson et al., 2021; Leaf et al., 2016; Cihon et al., 2021; Milne et al., 2017). In 2012, Leaf and colleagues conducted the first empirical investigation to teach three autistic individuals how to (1) interrupt; (2) change the game; (3) appropriate greetings; (4) joint attention; (5) changing the conversation; (6) abduction prevention; and (7) eye contact. The results of this study indicated that participants reached mastery criterion on 87.5% of skills. Since, this original study multiple studies have been conducted on teaching social interaction behaviors (i.e., compromising, sharing, and assertiveness) (Leaf et al., 2015); social communication skills (i.e., providing verbal support, chatting, and interrupting) (Milne et al., 2017); comparing the Cool versus Not Cool Procedure to Social Stories (Leaf, Mitchell, et al., 2016); and play skills (Leaf, Leaf, Milne, et al., 2016).

Although research has not directly evaluated the Cool versus Not Cool Procedure for teaching sexual education, it has been implemented clinically for several years and should be easily extended to skills related to the pursuit of romantic relationships. It is an appropriate procedure for any discrimination training that a learner may need. For example, the procedure could be used for teaching how to talk to someone else about your sexual orientation, how to communicate your needs, how to engage in appropriate hygiene and sexual hygiene, how to ask out someone, how to breakup with someone, or how to communicate with your partner. Essentially, if there is a discrimination that needs to be made, this is a wonderful program to teach the learner how to make the discrimination. It is important to remember, however, that the goal of the Cool versus Not Cool Procedure is not for the learner to just identify the correct discrimination but for them to display the appropriate behavior in their natural environment. This demonstration of the skill in the natural environment is the essential outcome.

Please note, however, that conversations related to sexuality are often associated with fear and with worry, and that they need to be approached with maximal sensitivity. It is also imperative that care be taken to understand the individual's environment, supports, and challenges. For example, one should never assume that an individual is ready to disclose their sexual identity or orientation, and should not make assumptions that such a disclosure is in their best interests. The provision of support is the most important element of care, and clinicians can provide a safe space to explore these and other conversations. It may even be the case that the clinician needs to educate the individual about risks of disclosure, so that they can explore together any consequences that might result from the disclosure and plan for appropriate timing, adequate support, and positive outcomes.

The teaching interaction procedure (TIP)

A third procedure that can be implemented to teach sexual education skills is the teaching interaction procedure. The teaching interaction procedure is a procedure that consists of both didactic instruction, demonstration, and role-playing. Although the teaching interaction procedure can be implemented for those students who are more impacted or who have less receptive or expressive language, it is ideally meant for those learners with high cognitive and language skills.

The first step of the teaching interaction procedure is for the practitioner to label and define the target behavior. For example, the practitioner might say: "Hey today we are going to talk about how you can talk to your parents about having independence on dates." Then, the practitioner has the learner repeat what they were going to talk about. For the purposes of instruction, let's consider an older adolescent negotiating with their parent that they would like to go on dates without being accompanied by a chaperone.

The second step is for the practitioner and the learner to come up with meaningful rationales of why the learner should display the behavior. This can be done by the practitioner stating one rationale and having the learner repeat the rationale or by the practitioner asking the learner to come with their own rationales. A rationale should be meaningful in that it reinforces the learner and encourages them to want to engage in the targeted behavior. Additionally, a good rationale usually takes the form of an "If ____ then _____ statement". For example, a good rationale might be: "If you tell your parents that you want to go on dates without a chaperone, it might make you feel more comfortable on dates and reduce your annoyance at your parents." A good rationale could also serve as a self-reminder of why a learner should engage in the behavior within the natural environment. Further, a good rationale will allow the practitioner to fade artificial reinforcement during teaching. Finally, a good rationale must be meaningful and individualized to the learner's needs and desires.

The third step of the teaching interaction procedure is breaking the targeted skill down into smaller behavioral components. In other words, a task analysis of the targeted behavior is created. For example, the practitioner might break the skill of revealing that you are gay to your parents into the following steps: (a) asking parents to talk; (b) finding a time to talk; (c) finding a place to talk; (d) stating what you want to talk about; (e) explaining that this is difficult to talk about; (f) stating what the boundaries are of the conversation; (g) stating what you want to tell them; and (h) attending to special considerations. The practitioner should break the skill down into as many steps as are needed for the learner to understand what they need to do in the natural environment. For some learners it will require more steps and for others it will require less steps. During the first teaching session, the practitioner will usually state the steps and have the learner repeat the steps. During subsequent sessions, the practitioner will just ask the learner to state the steps of the target behavior.

The fourth step of the teaching interaction procedure is the practitioner demonstrating the target behavior to the learner. This demonstration is identical to the demonstration in the Cool versus Not Cool Procedure. The fifth step of the teaching interaction procedure is the practitioner having the learner role-play the behavior. The role-play is also identical to the role-play component in the Cool versus Not Cool Procedure. The sixth and final step of the teaching interaction procedure is the provision of feedback. Feedback should include both positive reinforcement and corrective feedback. This reinforcement should be based upon how the learner does throughout the entire teaching interaction procedure, and should be delivered with sensitivity and compassion.

Finally, special considerations should be anticipated and embedded into instruction. In the case of this and other sexual skills, it is urgently important to attend to safety risks. In this case, unchaperoned dating might be reserved for circumstances where the dating partner is well-known. In addition, unchaperoned dating might be restricted to safe neighborhoods, and might not extend to the use of public transportation. Stages of independence can be planned, and there can be a gradual loosening of restrictions as skills develop, as time passes, and as experience accrues.

An important component of the teaching interaction procedure is for the practitioner to find ways to promote generalization for the learner. This can be done in numerous ways. First, the teaching interaction procedure should be implemented by multiple therapists. Second, the teaching interaction procedure should be implemented in different places and during different times. Third, the teaching interaction procedure should increase the provocativeness of the demonstration and role-play throughout the course of intervention. This can be done by making initial role-plays or demonstrations easy for the learner and gradually making it more and more like the natural environment. For example, the practitioner might start off by acting as a parent who asks no questions and agrees to changes in chaperoning. Over time, the parent may ask more difficult questions or respond not as positively.

The teaching interaction procedure was originally created as part of Achievement Place and the teaching family model (Phillips, 1971, 1974; Schumaker et al., 1983). Within the original conceptualization it was used to teach juvenile offenders or those at risk for juvenile offense to improve their behavior and overall quality of life (Phillips, 1971). Further, this procedure was adopted as part of the curriculum used in Boys Town (Dowd et al., 1994). The teaching interaction procedure has also been used clinically since the 1970s to teach autistic individuals a variety of behaviors including social skills, language development, adaptive behaviors, school readiness behaviors, reduction of aberrant behaviors, and sexual education. Finally, there has been a plethora of research conducted on the teaching interaction procedure for autistic individuals. This research has evaluated the procedure in a one-to-one instructional format (Leaf et al., 2010), a group instructional format (Dotson et al., 2010), compared to Social Stories (Leaf et al., 2012), improving social skills (Kassardjian et al., 2013), improving conversational skills (Dotson et al., 2010). The teaching interaction procedure can be used to teach any sexual educational skill, as it allows the learner to hear didactic information, watch a demonstration of the targeted skill, and practice the targeted behavior with the therapist. The procedure is collaborative, positive, and scaffolded. It is well-suited to teach the nuanced skills associated with pursuing relationships and expressing sexuality. Teaching interaction procedure is beneficial to teach skills related to dating; asking someone out on a date, making plans, or what to do when you get there. It may be used to work on skills related to recognizing consent or lack thereof, or how to demonstrate consent (or lack thereof). It can be used to teach these, and more, skills in broad way, but also in a nuanced way focusing on intent and nuance. The role-play component of TiP makes it an ideal teaching methodology for skills that focus on nonverbal components, body language, tone of voice, and gesture.

Behavioral skills training

A variation of the teaching interaction procedure that can also be used in sexual education is behavioral skills training (Sarokoff & Sturmey, 2004). The difference between the two procedures is that in behavioral skills training there is no provision of a rationale and that there is only an appropriate demonstration of the targeted behavior (i.e., no inappropriate demonstration of the targeted behavior). Otherwise, the implementation of behavioral skills training is identical to the teaching interaction procedure. Behavioral skills training has also been implemented for over 40 years to individuals with and without a diagnosis of autism spectrum disorder. Further, behavioral skills training has been one of the most evaluated procedures in the behavior analytic research. This procedure has been used to teach pedestrian safety skills (Harriage et al., 2016), social skills (Dogan et al., 2017), gun safety skills (Miltenberger et al., 2009), and language skills (Nuernberger et al., 2013). Behavioral skills training can be used to teach any sexual educational skill as it allows the learner to hear didactic information, watch a demonstration of the targeted skill, and practice the targeted behavior with the therapist. This procedure may be best for individuals who are confused by rationales or who perseverate on the demonstrations of errors. In either case (BST or TIP), there is a focus on systematically approaching complex skills with modeling, practice, and feedback.

Video modeling

Another procedure that can be used in sexual education for autistic/individuals diagnosed with ASD is video modeling (Charlop et al., 2010), sometimes referred to as video-based instruction (Cihak et al., 2012; Grosberg & Charlop, 2014; Gutierrez et al., 2016; LeBlanc et al., 2003; MacDonald et al., 2005; MacManus et al., 2015; Nikopoulous & Keenan, 2004; Plavnick et al., 2013; Travers & Tincani, 2010). In video modeling, the learner watches a video of how they should display the target behavior. Video modeling is beneficial for learners who have good attending skills and generalized imitation (McCoy & Hermansen, 2007). The practitioner should set up the video ahead of time and ensure that the video captures the correct demonstration of the targeted skill, preferably in the learner's natural environment. For example, if the targeted skill was breaking up with your significant other, the video should target this behavior in the environment where this is most likely to happen.

The practitioner has multiple choices in how to create the video. First, the practitioner needs to choose if the video is going to include actors or if the video will include the learner themselves. Second, the practitioner selects if they are going to film the targeted behavior like a movie or if they are going to film it from the point of view of the learner. Third, the practitioner decides what the focus of the scene is. Finally, the practitioner can determine how many different variations the video model will consist of. Additional variations can aid in the generality of the skill, and can also ensure that the individual does not learn one, unchanging script in the context of practice.

During video modeling the instructor tells the learner that they are going to watch a movie of the targeted behavior. Next, the learner watches the video in its entirety. Finally, the practitioner either asks comprehension questions at the end of the video or role-plays the behavior with the learner. The practitioner could also pause the movie at any time to highlight certain important aspects to the learner or to answer any questions the learner may have.

Video modeling has been used since the 1980s both in clinical practice and in research. Researchers have demonstrated it can be effective for teaching perspective skills (LeBlanc et al., 2003), requesting (Cihak et al.,

2012), novel play statements (MacManus et al., 2015), peer engagement (Grosberg & Charlop, 2014; Plavnick et al., 2013), play (MacDonald et al., 2005), and sexual education (Travers & Tincani, 2010). The improvements in technology have made video modeling easy to implement as it is easier to capture short videos in the moment. This procedure is great to teach a variety of sexual education skills. It should be noted, however, that we are not encouraging practitioners to show video models of how to engage in the act of sex (i.e., pornography) as there would be ethical, moral, and legal concerns. Instead, this is an additional procedure that has utility for practicing difficult conversations or behaviors associated with expressing interest or navigating conflict in dating. One of the benefits of video modeling is, especially when filmed like a movie, the video can show outcomes or reactions from all participants. For example, if using an interaction of people flirting, this allows the practitioner to show the body language, postures, language, and affect of both parties. This may help the learner identify what cues they can look for in their partner in future situations.

The general availability of smartphones has made video modeling incredibly accessible and easy to create. This allows for quick and very relevant models to be created, increasing the likelihood of their utility as a teaching tool.

Parent coaching

Despite the plethora of teaching procedures available, the content of some parts of sex education are, quite simply, not appropriate to be taught to an individual by a professional. The intimate and personal nature of much of the content of sex education makes it inaccessible and inappropriate to be taught directly by a professional. ABA has demonstrated much success using parent coaching models. This may be done using many of the same techniques outlined above. Parents can be trained to use methods like Cool versus Not Cool, or Behavioral Skills Training. Parent coaching may be as simple as demonstrating teaching with similar skills and explaining how parents would adapt that to a particular target (i.e., showing parents how they would model washing their torso, arms, legs, etc.), then explaining how to teach using similar strategies how to teach washing genitals to their child.

As well as using parent coaching to teach new skills, parents should be coached on the maintenance of skills being taught in other settings. For example, when teaching a functional "no" response, it is important that the rationale for this is explained to parents, and parents are also taught how to prompt and reinforce this skill in natural settings at home, as well as under what conditions they should and shouldn't teach the skill.

For some parents teaching sexuality skills is uncomfortable. Overall coaching should be given to parents in how to talk about and teach in a direct, clear way, as well as how to access further resources if needed to help with their content knowledge if required.

Social skills groups

The final intervention that can be used to teach autistic/individuals diagnosed with ASD about sexual behavior is social skills groups. Social skills groups are opportunities for three or more individuals to come together and work on a variety of behaviors simultaneously. Within social skills groups the practitioner can implement, and should implement, different behavioral analytic interventions including: discrete trial teaching, video modeling, script fading, the teaching interaction procedure, behavioral skills training, and the Cool versus Not Cool procedure. Further, the practitioner can teach a variety of different curricular programs. Implementing sexual education in a social skills group setting has many advantages for the learner. First, it puts learners in proximity to each other, which may increase the likelihood of friendship development and generalization of skills taught. Second, it is an efficient form of instruction as it allows for multiple learners to be taught simultaneously. Third, it allows for the opportunity to learn incidentally or through observational learning. Finally, it has been found to be highly effective in both clinical practice and with empirical studies (Akers et al., 2018; Garfinkle & Schwartz, 2002; Leaf, Leaf, McEachin, et al., 2016; Kassardjian et al., 2013; Leaf et al., 2010; Palmen et al., 2008; Wolfberg & Schuler, 1993). Social skills groups allow the practitioner to teach sexual educational goals as the practitioner can implement a variety of teaching procedures based upon the needs and strengths of the learners. Many skills related to sexuality are amenable to group teaching, and many of the above teaching strategies can be implemented in a group setting. Targets can include practicing both initiating and responding to various types of social initiations (conversations, sharing contact information, making plans), practicing socially appropriate distance, recognizing consent (in nonsexual situations), even working on online safety and online interactions. However, it is important that practitioners ensure that all members are comfortable talking about the topics in the group, that they have a way to leave the group at any time, and that members can be separated based upon certain topics.

Conclusion

This chapter provided you with a brief overview of different procedures that can be implemented to teach sexual education to autistic/individuals diagnosed with ASD. The interventions that are listed are not a comprehensive list as there are other procedures that can be used as well. These procedures can include script fading (Krantz & McClannahan, 1993), video prompting (Bennett et al., 2013), fluency instruction (Weiss, 2001), and pivotal response training (Koegel et al., 2014). Finally, within the curriculum portion of this book we will state what procedures are the most appropriate to teach the different sexual educational skills that are provided in the book. We encourage practitioners to use only those procedures that have empirical support, are considered to be evidence-based procedures, and are conceptually systematic with behavior analysis. As a final note, please remember the importance of assessing and planning for safety considerations in this area of instruction, and remember that mastery of skills depends entirely on transfer to naturally occurring contexts.

PART TWO

Curriculum

CHAPTER 4

Age ranges

Abstract

Throughout the curriculum portion of the book, each skill has suggested target ages to teach. Age ranges are unrelated to whether the individual is in school currently, rather refer to an age range. Appropriateness and need for skill will vary by individual and as such, these age recommendations should be regarded as guidelines.

Keywords: Adolescence; Adult; Age ranges; Early adolescence; Preschool; School age.

Throughout the curriculum portion of the book, each skill has suggested target ages to teach. *Age ranges are unrelated to whether the individual is in school currently, rather refer to an age range. Appropriateness and need for skill will vary by individual and as such, these age recommendations should be regarded as guidelines.*

The following are the age ranges outlined throughout.

Description	Ages
Preschool	3–5
School age	6–10
Early adolescence	11–14
Adolescence	15–20
Adult	21+

Clinician's Guide to Sexuality and Autism
ISBN 978-0-323-95743-4
https://doi.org/10.1016/B978-0-323-95743-4.00015-1

CHAPTER 5

Body parts

Abstract

This domain will target knowledge of body parts. Knowing and using the correct terminology for body parts is important to aid in communication to trusted adults and healthcare professionals; being able to talk about body parts that hurt or are otherwise unwell is essential. Additionally, being able to refer to body parts correctly is important as it pertains to being able to report inappropriate interactions as related to safety and abuse prevention.

Understanding and using slang for body parts also has importance; slang is used in most social interactions and without understanding this terminology the individual will be unable to participate in the interaction. It also means that if the individual doesn't understand the slang and the body part to which it refers, they will not be able to understand the terminology being used. As such, it is important to understand the stimulus equivalence of the correct terminology to any slang used in the individual's family or social communities.

Finally, an understanding of what type of language to use in what communicative settings is important to maintain appropriate and effective interactions.

Keywords: Autism; Body parts; Slang; Terminology.

Clinician's Guide to Sexuality and Autism
ISBN 978-0-323-95743-4
https://doi.org/10.1016/B978-0-323-95743-4.00014-X

Overall goal	• Using scientific/medically correct terminology, the individual can: ◦ If female, the individual can label the following parts on themselves and in pictures: breasts, buttocks, vagina, vulva, clitoris, and anus ◦ If female, the individual can label the following male body parts in pictures: penis, scrotum, anus, buttocks ◦ If male, the individual can label the following body parts on themselves and in pictures: penis, scrotum, anus, buttocks ◦ If male, the individual can label the following female body parts in picture: breasts, buttocks, vagina, vulva, clitoris, anus • The individual can demonstrate an understanding of culturally and contextually equivalent appropriate slang for breasts, vagina, penis, testicles, and buttocks
Teaching methodologies	Discrete Trial Teaching, Parent Coaching
Cross-referenced skills	Health and hygiene
Special considerations	Age and situation-appropriate slang changes will vary based on culture and social situations. Make sure that the informants for slang choices are within the population in which the learner will use the slang (i.e., ask teenagers what teenagers say, don't try to guess).

While identification of body parts may often be included in many teaching programs, typically they are either targeted too broadly and accurate labels for genitals are glossed over or may be avoided all together. Alternatively in traditional sex education programs all parts of the reproductive system may be targeted which may be overwhelming and not well maintained. The goal in this approach is a focus on functionality and meaningfulness for the learner. As such, it is important for learners to be able to use scientific and medically correct terminology to label body parts on themselves and in pictures. This may be used in conversation with parents, doctors, and other medical professionals, and others. Additionally, it is equally important that learners are familiar with culture, family, and socially used slang. Slang words for body parts are used differently within families, but also within different social settings. Understanding and using the correct slang in the correct contexts is important for social interactions—most kids and adolescents use slang and other casual language when talking about anything related to sexuality. As much as this is a social skill, it is also a safety skill—if there is a disconnect or misunderstanding related to the body part that is being spoken to, it can create confusion or even result in people being put in situations they were not expecting or understanding. Alternately, only using slang proficiently may result in poor, disjointed, or even offensive communication to parents, medical professionals, or other trusted adults.

When teaching slang, as with any other aspect of sexuality, even the best-intentioned parents and professionals may not be the best reference point. It is important to talk directly to the family members to find out if there are casual or other special names that they use when discussing body parts. Likewise, adults are, sadly, usually out of touch with the slang being used by children and teens; ensuring that the slang being taught is the terminology that is likely to actually be used by the learner is important. Finally, slang changes over time. Preschool aged children may use words like "pee pee" to mean "penis," whereas adolescents may be more likely to use something common like "dick" or even more silly like "hairy canary" or "love muscle." Ensuring that these are revisited and retaught over time and context changes is important.

Teaching body parts may typically be done using Discrete Trial Teaching. See Chapter 3 for further description of discrete trial teaching. Additionally, particular targets pertaining to identifying body parts on oneself should be taught by a parent or caregiver, not by a therapist of other professional. Being aware of the secondary skills that are being taught throughout is incredibly important; having a therapist or other professional in a private space teaching a label of one's penis on themselves may teach the learner to label their penis, but inadvertently may also teach the learner that it is acceptable to be in a private space with an unfamiliar adult. Using parent coaching strategies outlined in Chapter 3 can help guide clinicians in ways to work with parents so that parents can be the ones teaching their children to label their own genitals. Modeling how to teach other body parts or using a Behavioral Skills Training technique will help parents understand how to teach more private body parts effectively. Clinicians must address this with parents/caregivers though and not assume that parents/caregivers will teach these parts, also ensuring that both "family" slang and correct terminology is taught.

At all ages, both the scientifically correct terminology and the age-appropriate slang should be taught. Additionally at older ages, if slang has changed for targets previously learned, teaching should update to this as well.

Using as realistic and accurate photos as possible is important for teaching, as well as multiple exemplars of each body part. Remember that body parts look different on different people and should be representative of as many samples as possible; genitals with and without pubic hair, circumcised and uncircumcised penises, etc.

Finally, the temptation may be there to teach a lot of nuanced parts of the reproductive system (remember grade 7 health class worksheets!). This will be addressed further in the chapter on reproduction, but the guiding principle should be on functionality for the learner. What skills do the learner require to be safe, to be happy, to engage in social interactions? Those should be targeted first and only if and when those are acquired skills should one move on to teach less directly impactful ones. Its more important to be able to label your own penis and scrotum, than it is to label the vas deferens on a diagram.

By preschool age individuals should be learning to:

- o Identify on themselves (biologically female) using technical language and slang
  - Vagina
  - Bum
- o Identify on themselves (biologically male) using technical language and slang
  - Penis
  - Scrotum
  - Bum

By school age individuals should be learning to:

- o Identify on themselves (biologically female) using technical language and slang
  - Breasts

By early adolescence individuals should be learning to:

- o Identify on themselves (biologically female) using technical language and slang
  - Vulva
  - Clitoris
  - Buttocks
  - Anus
- o Identify in pictures (all) using technical language and slang
  - Penis
  - Scrotum
  - Breasts
  - Vagina
  - Vulva
  - Clitoris

Body parts—bio

Skill one	The biologically female individual can receptively and expressively identify the following body parts on themself and in pictures using clinically correct names: **o** Vagina **o** Bum	Preschool
Skill two	The biologically male individual can receptively and expressively identify the following body parts on themself and in pictures using clinically correct names: **o** Penis **o** Scrotum **o** Bum	Preschool
Skill three	The biologically female individual can receptively and expressively identify the following body parts on themself and in pictures using clinically correct names: **o** Breasts	School age
Skill four	The biologically female individual can receptively and expressively identify the following body parts on themself and in pictures using clinically correct names: **o** Vulva **o** Clitoris **o** Buttocks **o** Anus The biologically female individual can identify the following body parts in pictures: **o** Penis **o** Scrotum The biologically male individual can identify the following body parts on themselves and in pictures: **o** Buttocks The biologically male individual can label the following female body parts in pictures: **o** Breasts **o** Buttocks **o** Vagina **o** Vulva **o** Clitoris **o** Anus	Early adolescence
Teaching format	DTT	
Special considerations	Accurate photos should be used as often as possible in teaching (as opposed to drawings or sketches of body parts). Ensure that multiple exemplars are used of each part as necessary (e.g., circumcised and uncircumcised penis, genitals with and without pubic hair).	

Body parts—slang

Skill one	The biologically female individual can receptively and expressively identify the following body parts on themself and in a picture using age-appropriate slang body parts names: **o** Vagina **o** Bum	Preschool
Skill two	The biologically male individual can receptively and expressively identify the following body parts on themself and in pictures using age-appropriate slang body part names: **o** Penis **o** Scrotum **o** Bum	Preschool
Skill three	The biologically female individual can receptively and expressively identify the following body parts on themself and in pictures using age-appropriate slang body parts names: **o** Breasts	School age
Skill four	The biologically female individual can receptively and expressively identify the following body parts on themself and in a picture using age-appropriate **slang** body parts names: **o** Vulva **o** Clitoris **o** Buttocks **o** Anus The biologically female individual can identify the following body parts in pictures: **o** Penis **o** Scrotum The biologically male individual can identify the following body parts on themselves and in pictures: **o** buttocks The male individual can label the following female body parts in picture: breasts, buttocks, vagina, vulva, clitoris, and anus	
Early adolescence		
Teaching format	DTT	
Special considerations	Slang should be age-referenced to peers within this specified age group. Additionally, slang should include any slang that the family uses or is common within the learner's culture.	

CHAPTER 6
Menstrual care

Abstract

This domain will target skills related to effective menstrual care. Skills in this domain should be targeted early, as in some cases, tolerating menstrual products may take some time. Independence should be prioritized and, as such, great individualization may be required. Adaptations may include teaching to change menstrual products on a time-based interval as opposed to teaching the discrimination of when a product should be changed, using period underwear instead of other products, and using visual supports.

Keywords: Autism; Menstrual care; Menstrual cups; Pantyliners; Period; Sanitary supplies; Tampons.

Overall goal	• The individual identifies the onset of her period • The individual uses appropriate products at appropriate times within their cycle (e.g., extra-absorbent for heavy days, tampons if swimming, etc.) • The individual can independently select, change, and dispose of sanitary pads, pantyliners, menstrual cups, and/or tampons in private • The individual carries pads, tampons, and pantyliners on them when they will be needed • The individual monitors their stock of sanitary supplies, and purchases or requests more in advance of needing them • The individual tracks their menstrual cycle
Teaching methodologies	Discrete Trial Teaching, Video Modeling, Parent Coaching
Special considerations	Ongoing considerations for independence should be prioritized here. It is important that teaching in this area begin far in advance for menses as tolerance to sanitary materials can sometimes be lengthy.
Cross-referenced skills	This domain closely aligns with health and hygiene, as well as preferences.

Clinician's Guide to Sexuality and Autism
ISBN 978-0-323-95743-4
https://doi.org/10.1016/B978-0-323-95743-4.00008-4

Menstruation is an unavoidable part of adulthood for women, and this is not different for women on the autism spectrum. Menstruation can affect women in many ways, including the impact of hormonal shifts on mood, behavior, and even appetite and sleep patterns. Like most areas of sexuality instruction, it is important to begin teaching in this area early, long before the onset of menses. In some cases, tolerance to wearing a pantyliner or pad may be lengthy to establish. For others, teaching independent management of sanitary materials may take some time. Targeting these skills in advance of when they are needed will mean a smoother transition to independence once the individual begins menses.

Independence in this area is vital. Hopefully by this point in life, the learner is already consistently independent in toileting and washroom skills. If we do not teach menstrual care to independence then we sacrifice prior teaching in washroom independence; requiring assistance with menstrual care means the individual is still in a vulnerable position with an adult in the washroom with them on a regular basis. As such, independence in menstrual care is a safety skill. Throughout this chapter, independence in skill should be prioritized over complexity of skill. As such, the goal should be to teach the skill at as complex or advanced level possible while maintaining independence in responding. Some learners will be able to try different types of menstrual products (e.g., pads, tampons, menstrual cup, etc.), choose which they like best, and independently acquire and use these. For others, tolerating a sanitary pad or learning how to use a tampon may be an insurmountable challenge. It may be preferable in these cases to teach the learner to wear period underwear instead.

When considering to what degree the individual can manage their own menstrual care we need to consider skills like monitoring when to change their pad/tampon/menstrual cup, choosing between preferred items, and monitoring their stock of sanitary supplies, procuring more in advance of need. Trying different types of menstrual products overlaps here with preferences and helps individuals decide what type and brand of product they like best.

Finally, it is also important that the individual is able to accurately track their period, and report this to appropriate individuals (e.g., caregiver, doctor) as needed.

Menstrual care can be taught using Discrete Trial Teaching, Video Modeling, and Parent Coaching. As always, teaching should be individualized per learner. See Chapter 3 for further description of teaching procedures.

By early adolescence individuals should be learning to:

- Tolerate wearing a pantyliner or pad
- Independently change and dispose of pantyliner or pad as needed. If not able to tolerate pad or pantyliner, OR is not independently able to manage changing a pad or pantyliner after reasonable instructional attempts period underwear could be considered as an alternative. Period underwear may also be considered for use while teaching.
- Carry pad, pantyliner, and or tampons with them for when they will be needed.
- Identify the onset of her period
- Track her period using a calendar, electronic, or other methods

By adolescence individuals should be learning to:

- Independently and privately change and dispose of tampons as needed
- Independently change and clean menstrual cups as needed
- Monitor their stock of sanitary supplies and purchase or request more in advance of needing them
- Use appropriate products at appropriate times within their cycle
- Identify the onset of PMS symptoms and how to manage them
- Recognize and demonstrate understanding of health concerns related to missed or irregular periods and can report to the appropriate person

Management of sanitary materials

Skill one	The individual tolerates wearing pantyliner or pad	Early adolescence
Skill two	The individual independently changes and disposes of pantyliner, and pad as needed	Early adolescence
Skill one and two alternative	If the individual is not able to tolerate (after reasonable instructional attempts) pad or pantyliner, OR is unable to independently manage changing a pad or pantyliner consider the use of period underwear (i.e.,. knix, Thinx, etc.). Period underwear can also be used if insufficient time was allocated to teaching tolerance of a particular product(s), while the learner is working to acquire the skill.	Early adolescence
Skill three	The individual carries pads, pantyliners, and/or tampons with them when they will be needed (note: discrimination of when needed is not required for this skill).	Early adolescence
Skill four (optional)	The individual independently and privately changes and disposes of tampons as needed.	Adolescence
Skill five (optional)	The individual independently changes and cleans menstrual cups as needed.	Adolescence
Skill six	The individual monitors their stock of sanitary supplies and purchases or requests more in advance of needing them.	Adolescence
Skill seven	The individual uses appropriate products at appropriate times within their cycle (e.g., extra absorbent for heavy days, etc.).	Adolescence
Teaching format	Video modeling, parent coaching, DTT	
Special considerations	Skills one and two—this could take a varying amount of time depending on the learner. Starting this process should begin no later than the earliest signs of puberty.	

Tracking of cycle

Skill one	The individual identifies the onset of her period.	Early adolescence
Skill two	The individual tracks her period using a calendar, electronic or other method.	Early adolescence
Skill three	The individual identifies the onset of PMS symptoms and how to manage them.	Adolescence
Skill four	The individual recognizes and demonstrates understanding of health concerns (pregnancy, other health issues) related to missed or irregular periods and can report to the appropriate person	Adolescence
Teaching format	Video modeling, parent coaching, DTT	

CHAPTER 7

Reproduction and birth control

Abstract

This domain covers skills related to reproduction and birth control. An understanding of reproduction and birth control is important to help protect against Sexually Transmitted Infections (STIs) and unwanted pregnancy, as well as understanding how to get pregnant should this be desired. Skills in this area include an understanding of the process of reproduction, identification and use of different forms of birth control, and the purchasing and storage of birth control.

Keywords: Autism; Birth control; Contraceptive; Reproduction; Sexually transmitted infections.

Overall goal	• The individual can describe the process of reproduction including a demonstrated understanding of the following processes: ovulation, intercourse, ejaculation • The individual can identify and use different forms of birth control, as relevant for protection against unwanted pregnancy and/or STI/STDs. • The individual can purchase and safely store birth control to have available when needed (if necessary)
Teaching methodologies	Discrete Trial Teaching, Teaching Interaction Procedure, Behavioral Skills Training, Parent Coaching
Cross reference	Sexual acts, body parts, health and hygiene
Special considerations	Maintaining personal autonomy and preference needs to be prioritized throughout this teaching. This closely aligns with body parts, preferences, sexual acts, and health and hygiene domains.

While including a domain on reproduction and birth control in a curriculum about sexuality is probably obvious, the way in which it should be taught is again slightly different to other approaches. Like teaching about body parts and puberty, teaching about reproduction and birth control

Clinician's Guide to Sexuality and Autism
ISBN 978-0-323-95743-4
https://doi.org/10.1016/B978-0-323-95743-4.00017-5

should take a learner-centered, applied approach. Those skills that are directly relevant to the learner should be the focus. When learning about the reproductive system, a functional applied approach should be taken, ensuring that the learner is able to label and describe parts that are most needed in their life at the time to mastery before moving on in teaching to those that are more complex.

Understanding reproduction and many skills related to birth control are skills that support safety of the individual by preventing STI's and unwanted pregnancy, but also the autonomy of the individual by teaching about different types of birth control and helping to establish preference.

This is also a domain with close cross-reference to Individual Preferences. Understanding types of birth control, what each type does (and does not do) helps individuals make informed choices about what type they want to use. Choice is an important part of autonomy and thus needs to be a consideration in all parts of teaching.

Reproduction and Birth Control can be taught using Discrete Trial Teaching, Teaching Interaction Procedure, Behavioral Skills Training, and Parent Coaching. For further description of these please see Chapter 3 and as always individualize per learner. As is the case with many skills, skills related to birth control use should be taught in advance of the individual becoming sexually active to allow time for acquisition of skill.

By school age individuals should be learning to:

- Identify and label parts of the reproductive system in picture/diagram.

By early adolescence individuals should be learning to:

- Describe the reproductive system in terms of sequence of events, and function of each component.
- Identify and describe different forms of birth control.
- Describe what each type of birth control protects against (e.g., STD, pregnancy).
- Describe or demonstrate on a prop where applicable how to use various forms of birth control.

By adolescence individuals should be learning to:

- Purchase or otherwise procure preferred forms of birth control.
- Safely store birth control and ensure they have adequate supply available.
- Manage the logistic components of birth control (e.g., renewing prescriptions, checking expiry dates).
- Carry needed birth control to use when needed.
- Discuss birth control with sexual partner as needed and appropriate.

Reproductive system

Skill one	The individual can identify and label parts of the reproductive system in picture/diagram	School age
Skill two	The individual can describe the reproductive system in terms of sequence of events, and function of each component	Early adolescence
Teaching format	DTT	
Special considerations	Skills one and two—this could take a varying amount of time depending on the learner. Instruction should begin no later than the earliest signs of puberty	

Birth control

Skill one	The individual can identify and describe different forms of birth control	Early Adolescence
Skill two	The individual describes what each type of birth control protects against (STD, pregnancy, etc.)	Early adolescence
Skill three	The individual can describe or demonstrate on a prop (where appropriate) how to use various forms of birth control	Early adolescence
Skill four	The individual can purchase or otherwise procure preferred forms of birth control	Adolescence
Skill five	The individual can safely store birth control and ensure they have adequate supply available	Adolescence
Skill six	The individual can manage the logistic components of birth control (e.g., checking expiry dates, taking pill regularly, renewing prescription)	Adolescence
Skill seven	The individual carries needed birth control (including a barrier method if currently using a pill) to use when needed	Adolescence
Skill eight	The individual discusses birth control with sexual partners as needed and appropriate	Adolescence
Teaching format	DTT, TIP, BST	
Special considerations	The age ranges for these skills are guidelines/suggestions only. Many of these skills are relevant once an individual is sexually active which varies. It is important that the skills are taught in advance of this with sufficient time allowance to learn the skills	

CHAPTER 8
Health and hygiene

Abstract

Health and hygiene are important as sexuality domain, both for personal safety and for an individual's overall dignity and quality of life. From a safety lens, the more independent an individual is in self-care, the lower the need will be for any paid assistance. As such, independence in this domain should be targeted early.

In terms of personal health management, it is important that individuals develop a sense of autonomy to the greatest extent possible. The private nature of a person's sexuality means that it is important for the individual to recognize normal or abnormal changes in their body or in individual health patterns, and to take the correct steps to remedy it (even if those steps are only telling a trusted adult).

Keywords: Autism; Health; Hygiene; Monitors health; Puberty; Signs of puberty; Tolerates medical procedures.

Overall goal	• The individual can maintain appropriate hygiene including washing self and keeping genitals clean • The individual regularly checks for, and can monitor warning signs of any health concerns and can report these to an appropriate person (i.e., makes doctor appointment, tells caregiver, conducts self-assessments, etc.) • The individual is tolerant of medical exams including (as appropriate): breast exams, pap tests or other gynecological exams, exams of penis and scrotum, blood draws
Teaching methodologies	Discrete Trial Teaching, Cool vs. Not Cool, Teaching Interaction Procedure, Behavioral Skills Training, Video Modeling, Parent Coaching
Cross-referenced skills	This area cross-references with social skills, body parts, and menstrual care
Special considerations	Independence in this area should be highlighted as a priority. High levels of independence in these skills enhances dignity and reduces the likelihood of victimization

Clinician's Guide to Sexuality and Autism
ISBN 978-0-323-95743-4
https://doi.org/10.1016/B978-0-323-95743-4.00004-7

At first, considerations regarding health and hygiene may not seem to be a sexuality skill. Independence throughout health and hygiene routines serves as a safety skill, helping protect individuals against potentially abusive situations. Individuals that can complete hygiene routines independently require less assistance from unfamiliar people or paid staff members in vulnerable situations; if you can shower independently, you don't require an adult in the bathroom with you while you are naked. Independence throughout personal care routines is also important to promote and maintain dignity of individuals with autism. As individuals are interested in dating and relationships, hygiene may also contribute to social interactions. Finally, a consideration of optional hygiene skills (e.g., hair removal if desired) is included.

It is important for individuals with autism to manage medical routines well and calmly. We recognize that many of the sexual health practices are invasive, intrusive, and can also cause physical discomfort. While these practises are often challenging to create teaching opportunities around, it is important that individuals are not experiencing them for the first time as adults, in unfamiliar settings, or in those occasioned by trauma.

Puberty is important to be targeted with individuals on the spectrum, but with a self-centered focus. While it is optimal for everyone to understand all the components of puberty in people of both sexes, the most important thing is for one to understand what is happening to their own body. Focusing on this first and ensuring understanding of these changes happening to themselves will help ensure safety, and anxiety about their body. Only at this point should puberty in others be introduced.

Finally, this domain includes monitoring oneself. As individuals further develop independence in self-care, other adults will have less time monitoring their bodies and as such are more likely to miss signs of abnormality. Reporting signs of abnormality, as well as feelings of unwellness should be targets.

This domain can be taught using Discrete Trial Teaching, Cool versus Not Cool, Teaching Interaction Procedures, Behavioral Skills Training, Video Modeling, or Parent Coaching. See Chapter 3 for further description of these.

Finally, skills in this domain should be taught with an emphasis on independence and individual comfort. When teaching skills about health, it is most important to emphasize completion independently over perfection. This may be accounted for by being adaptive in mastery; for instance, a "good enough" shower every day can be complemented with a thorough shower with assistance from a trusted caregiver once weekly. In terms of tolerance to health procedures, teaching these gradually, systematically, and in such a way that the individual remains calm and continues to assent to procedures is of utmost importance. In some cases this means that teaching progresses slowly and thus these should begin early. As well, while all of these skills are important, some of them occur at a very low frequency. This may mean maintenance of skills is challenging for some learners, which should be considered.

At preschool age individuals should be learning to:

- Tolerate a bath or shower including a parent/guardian-assisted washing of all body parts

At school age individuals should be learning to:

- Tolerate a bath and a shower including parent/guardian-assisted washing of all body parts.
- Wash (with prompting) their:
  - Hair
  - Face
  - Body
  - Armpits
  - Penis/vagina
  - Buttocks and anus
  - Legs and feet
- Brush their hair independently
- Brush their teeth independently
- Tolerate routine doctor visits including:
  - Doctor touching their body
  - Doctor measuring their height and weight
  - Doctor listening to their chest
  - Doctor looking at eyes, ears, and throat
- Recognize what their own body parts usually look like and can report small abnormalities like scratches or insect bites
- Report feeling unwell and give specifics regarding body parts that hurt or feel uncomfortable

At early adolescence individuals should be learning to:

- Complete all steps of a shower or bathing routine independently including turning the water on/running a bath at appropriate temperature and washing all body parts independently.
- Safely engage in appropriate hair removal techniques as desired.
- Be tolerant of blood draws

- Be tolerant of various medical settings including clinics and hospitals
- Be tolerant of pap tests, gynecological exams and breast exams (females), and exams of the penis and scrotum (males).
- Recognize irregularities in menstrual cycles and any abnormalities in genitals or discharge
- Recognize the following signs of puberty in themselves:
  - Females:
    - Breast development
    - Hair in underarms and genitals
    - Vaginal discharge and menstruation
  - Males
    - Hair growth on face, underarms, and genitals
    - Growth of testicles and penis
    - Voice changes

At adolescence individuals should be learning to:

- Monitor, make, and attend regular health check up appointments
- Conduct regular breast exams (female)
- Conduct regular testicular exams (male)

Hygiene

Skill one	The individual can tolerate a bath or shower including parent/guardian-assisted washing of all body parts	Preschool
Skill two	The individual can tolerate a bath and a shower including parent/guardian-assisted washing of all body parts. The individual may prefer a bath or a shower, but is able to tolerate either if necessary	School age
Skill three	The individual can wash the following body parts (with prompting): o Hair o Face o Body o Armpits o Penis/Vagina o Buttocks and anus o Legs and feet	School age
Skill four	The individual can brush their hair independently	School age
Skill five	The individual can brush their teeth independently	School age
Skill six	The individual can complete all steps of shower or bathing routine independently including turning the water on/running a bath at appropriate temperature, and washing all body parts independently	Early adolescence
Skill seven	The individual can safely engage in appropriate hair removal techniques (i.e., shaving, waxing, cream, etc.) as desired.	Early adolescence
Teaching format	Parent coaching, DTT, TIP, BST, Cool not Cool	
Special considerations	Independent skill consideration: Independence in hygiene skills is a safety skill. For clients that are unable to complete washing all body parts sufficiently consider the following: - Prioritize washing armpits, genitals, and anus over the rest of the body - Teaching client to independently wash "good enough" most days, with a trusted adult assisting once a week	

Tolerates medical procedures

Skill one	The individual can tolerate routine doctor visits including: o Doctor touching their body o Doctor measuring height and weight o Doctor listening to chest o Doctor looking at eyes, ears, throat	School age
Skill two	The individual is tolerant of the following medical procedures: o Blood draw	Early adolescence
Skill three	The individual is tolerant of various medical settings including clinics and hospitals	Early adolescence
Skill four	Female: o The individual is tolerant of pap test and other gynecological exams o The individual is tolerant of breast exams Male: o The individual is tolerant of exams of the penis and scrotum	Early adolescence
Teaching format	Parent coaching, DTT, BST, TIP, Cool not Cool	
Special considerations	Tolerance skills may require ongoing assessment teaching to maintain. For many skills, the frequency of required demonstration based on medical need may be insufficient to ensure maintenance of skill. This will vary by learner and by skill and should be assessed for each individual. Tolerance may look different for all learners, but is defined here as: the individual remains in the presence of the medical professional throughout the procedure, does not attempt to leave the medical setting throughout the procedure, and refrains from engaging in any behavior that interferes with the practitioner's ability to complete the procedure.	

Monitors health

Skill one	The individual can recognize what their own body parts usually look like and can report small abnormalities—i.e., dirt, insect bites, small scratches, etc.	School age
Skill two	The individual can report feeling unwell, and give specifics regarding body parts that hurt or feel uncomfortable	School age
Skill three	The individual can recognize irregularities in menstrual cycles, and any abnormalities in their genitals (i.e., lumps), or discharge	Early adolescence
Skill four	The individual monitors, makes, and attends regular health check-up appointments	Adolescence
Skill five	The individual (female) conducts regular breast exams	Adolescence
Skill six	The individual (male) conducts regular testicular exams	Adolescence
Teaching format	Parent coaching, DTT, BST, TIP	
Special considerations	Prioritization of independence in these areas may require the use of tools (i.e., teaching tools for menstruation tracking—calendar or app), or adaptation (i.e., attending doctor appointments for physical check-ups is more important than making them independently).	

Puberty

Skill one	The individual can recognize the signs of puberty in themselves as applicable including: o Females: - Breast development - Hair in underarms and genitals - Vaginal discharge and menstruation o Males: - Hair growth on face, underarms, and genitals - Growth of testicles and penis - Voice changes	Early adolescence
Teaching format	Parent coaching, DTT, BST, TIP, Cool not Cool	
Special considerations	While it is important to be aware of changes due to puberty in the opposite sex as well as their own, priority should be placed on changes to their own body first before those of others	

CHAPTER 9

Sexuality and the law

Abstract

This domain covers skills pertaining to the law. For good reason, laws related to sexual acts are strict. This domain covers skills relating to awareness of, and obeying laws related to age of consent, pornography, public sexual acts, and assault. It is important to note that laws vary by jurisdiction and those teaching them should be aware of the law in the geographic settings relevant to their learner.

Keywords: Autism; Jurisdiction; Law; Pornography; Public sexual acts.

Overall goal	The individual is: • Aware of and follows laws related to age of consent (both in themselves and in partners) • Aware of and follows laws related to production, possession, and distribution of pornographic material • Aware of and follows laws related to public sexual acts • Aware of and follows laws related to assault including the perspective of the perpetrator and the victim
Teaching methodologies	Discrete Trial Teaching, Teaching Interaction Procedure, Behavioral Skills Training, Parent Coaching
Special considerations	Specific laws will vary by jurisdiction. Clinicians and educators should be familiar with the laws in their specific location and any other locations in which the learner may spend time
Cross-referenced skills	This area is closely aligned with consent, sexual abuse prevention and reporting; and online activity

An important aspect of teaching about sexuality is the prevelance and impact of errors. In almost all other aspects of teaching, some error is allowable in learning, and sometimes even within mastery—we don't always perform every skill in our repertoire with 100% accuracy all the time. In terms of sexuality however, the law is very clear and sexual misconduct is

Clinician's Guide to Sexuality and Autism
ISBN 978-0-323-95743-4
https://doi.org/10.1016/B978-0-323-95743-4.00016-3

(rightfully) punishable by law. It is important to understand this often black and white nature of the law and ensure that teaching this relality is included for learners with autism.

While not exhaustive, teaching about the law should cover areas of age of consent; laws related to production, possession, and distribution of pornography; public sexual acts, and assault. It is extremely important that learners are aware of the law, and understand what falls in and outside of each type of law. Ignorance of the law is rarely an excuse that holds up, and it is extremely important that learners understand which laws apply to them and in what ways.

To further complicate, laws may vary across jurisdiction; it is important that those teaching people with ASD are aware of the laws in the jurisdiction that the learner currently resides, as well as any the learner is likely to encounter. If moving to or visiting within another jurisdiction it is important to update teaching on the laws that apply.

It is important that the severity of consequences is highlighted to learners, and that every effort is taken to ensure understanding of the magnitude and severity of consequences of breaking the law.

This domain can be taught using Discrete Trial Teaching, Parent Coaching. Teaching Interaction Procedure, Behavioral Skills Training. For further description of these, please see Chapter 3. As always, individualization of teaching per learner is required.

By adolescence individuals should be learning to:

- State the age of consent for engaging in sexual acts, including any variability across types of sexual act
- Identify if they are within the age of consent
- Describe the types and variations of acts that are included in consent laws from the perspective of the victim
- Identify when familiar people are above the age of consent
- Can provide a reasonable description of the types and variations of such acts that are included under consent laws from the perspective of the perpetrator
- Demonstrate an understanding of the laws related to possession of pornography (including pornography that includes minors)
- Demonstrate an understanding of the laws regarding ownership and/or distribution of pornography
- Demonstrate an understanding of the laws related to acquisition of pornography including all media forms
- Demonstrate an understanding of the laws related to sexual acts in public places

- Demonstrate an understanding of the laws governing unwanted behavior or interactions (e.g., exposing oneself, stalking, etc.)
- Demonstrate an understanding of outdated laws that may be rarely enforced.

Laws as a victim

Skill one	The individual can state the age of consent for engaging in sexual acts, including any variability across types of sexual act	Adolescence
Skill two	The individual can identify if they are in the age of consent	Adolescence
Skill three	The individual can describe the types and variations of acts that are included under consent laws from the perspective of the victim	Adolescence
Teaching format	Parent coaching, DTT	
Special considerations	Age of consent varies based on jurisdiction. Additionally, it is important to teach to various sexual acts, even if the client is not currently demonstrating interest in particular acts	

Laws as a Perpetrator

Skill one	The individual can state the age of consent for engaging in sexual acts, including any variability across acts	Adolescence
Skill two	The individual can identify when familiar people are above the age of consent	Adolescence
Skill three	The individual can provide a reasonable description of the types, and variations, of such acts that are included under consent laws from the perspective of the perpetrator	Adolescence
Teaching format	Parent coaching, DTT	
Special considerations	Age of consent varies based on jurisdiction. Additionally, it is important to teach to various sexual acts, even if the client is not currently demonstrating interest in particular acts	

Laws related to pornography

Skill one	The individual demonstrates an understanding of the laws regarding possession of pornography (including pornography that includes minors)	Adolescence
Skill two	The individual demonstrates an understanding of the laws regarding ownership and/or distribution of pornography	Adolescence
Skill three	The individual demonstrates an understanding of laws related to acquisition of pornography including all media forms	Adolescence
Teaching format	Parent coaching, DTT	
Special considerations	It is important that this area covers acquisition of pornography in various forms/ways to access. It is also important that all aspects of pornography are covered in this domain (including sharing of photos of known people)	

Laws related to public acts

Skill one	The individual demonstrates an understanding of the laws regarding sexual acts in public places	Adolescence
Special considerations		

CHAPTER 10

Online activity

Abstract

This domain covers skills related to safety when engaging in online activity. The prevalence of online activity continues to increase and is obviously not going away anytime soon. Teaching safe online activity early is important. This section addresses skills in navigation and safe use of apps and websites, and safe sharing of personal information (textual and photos). This domain includes skills on safe and legal streaming and downloading of content online, as well as skills related to unwanted solicitations from others.

Keywords: Autism; Internet safety; Online activity; Online navigation; Privacy; School interactions.

Overall goal	• The individual can navigate and safely use dating apps/websites • The individual can demonstrate safe and legal streaming and downloading of sexual content • The individual demonstrates understanding of safe sharing of personal information including texting and photo sharing including recognition of solicitation of sexual imagery and information. • The individual can recognize when they are being sent inappropriate sexual solicitations or unwanted photos and blocks the sender
Teaching methodologies	Discrete Trial Teaching, Cool vs. Not Cool, Teaching Interaction Procedure, and Behavioral Skills Training
Special considerations	Online safety includes practice with age and socially appropriate online activity. It is important to teach these in consultation with peer groups in regard to what similar aged peers are actually playing. Additionally, families may have rules and restrictions around online access which should be addressed and honored where applicable
Cross-referenced skills	This domain closely aligns with law and social skills. Victimization is common for autistic individuals, and it is essential that they are educated about self-protection

Clinician's Guide to Sexuality and Autism
ISBN 978-0-323-95743-4
https://doi.org/10.1016/B978-0-323-95743-4.00009-6

Accessing information on the internet is a fast changing, and scary domain! While it is tempting to lean on parental controls and website/app restrictions to manage behavior in this area, this usually proves unsuccessful. Many children and adolescents are more adept with parental controls and their workarounds than the adults who set the controls so can often find ways to circumvent restrictions. Alternatively, they may encounter computers/phones/tablets in other settings where these restrictions are not in place. The fact is, internet is the most accessible it has ever been, and accessibiliy is likely to expand. As such, the safer approach is to teach individuals skills about safe and appropriate internet use.

Internet safety should be taught in website use, apps, and online gaming. All of these formats work a little bit differently and safety risks may be slightly different in each. It is likely that individuals will access all of these at some point and so all should be taught. As well, both the available apps/games/website activity changes over time, as will the individual's interest. Safety risks in used formats should be revisited regularly.

Safety risks may include (but are not limited to) accessing illegal content, solicitations of sexual content (e.g., requests to send photos), unwanted photos of others being sent, requests for personal information including credit card numbers. It can be challenging to discern some of these risks when engaging in interactions online, and puts people with autism at particular risk for victimization. While these risks may seem high and overwhelming, it is important to balance these with the fact that online activity provides important social opportunities. Many people use online means for social interactions and communication, leisure, and dating apps, and it is virtually impossible to avoid the benefits of online activity. For people on the autism spectrum who may not have the same access to peer groups and friends as others, this community is often found online. This can provide such important opportunities for social interaction, and shouldn't be avoided. Navigation and use of many different types of apps, games, and online sites should be included in teaching from a young age to help develop skills needed to access these sources of potential social interactions.

Online activity can be taught using Discrete Trial Teaching, Teaching Interaction Procedure, Behavioral Skills Training, and Cool versus Not Cool. See Chapter 3 for a further description of these teaching procedures, and always ensure teaching is individualized to the learner.

By school age individuals should be learning to:

- Demonstrate basic privacy rules while on an electronic device including:

  - o Being clothed while using device
  - o Refraining from taking device into the bathroom

By early adolescence individuals should be learning to:

- Refrain from sharing personal information with strangers online
- Demonstrate an understanding of, and use appropriately location services in apps
- Refrain from sharing photos of his/herself online
- Refrain from sharing photos of others online without their permission
- Understand that when photos are shared with permission that photos need to be appropriate
- Recognize unwanted or inappropriate solicitations for sexual imagery, conversations, and information
- Demonstrate functional and effective protest to unwanted or inappropriate solicitations for sexual imagery, conversations, and information
- Connect with known peers in games/apps including sharing contact information
- Use appropriate language in online chat forums
- Refrain from bullying when participating in online forums
- Create, use, and safely store appropriate usernames and passwords for online accounts
- Independently access and use email
- Proficiently and safely use age-appropriate social media
- Proficiently and safely uses age-appropriate online games

By adolescence individuals should be learning to:

- Select appropriate apps, social media, and games and reflect their own interest and comfort
- Initiate and respond to online flirting behavior (e.g., photos) from known individuals as desired and appropriate. This includes selection of photos that may be flirty or risqué without being pornographic or incongruent with the situation
- Initiate and respond to online flirting behavior (e.g., verbal) from known individuals as appropriate and desired. This includes flirting messages that match the situation
- Demonstrate an understanding of the various privacy and sharing settings on each app/site they use
- Demonstrate an understanding of navigation within various apps (e.g., swiping to respond)
- Demonstrate an understanding of the risks of downloading from various sites (e.g., costs, virus risk, distribution of personal information)

Privacy

Skill one	The individual demonstrates basic privacy rules while on an electronic device including: - Being clothed while using device - Refraining from taking device into bathroom	School age
Skill two	The individual refrains from sharing personal info (full name, address, school) with strangers online	Early adolescence
Skill three	The individual demonstrates an understanding, and uses appropriately, location services in apps	Early adolescence
Skill four	The individual refrains from sharing photos of his or herself online	Early adolescence
Skill five	The individual refrains from sharing photos of friends online without their permission	Early adolescence
Skill six	The individual understands that when photos are shared (with permission), that the photos need to be appropriate (no nudity, no private places, etc.)	Early adolescence
	The individual recognizes unwanted or inappropriate solicitations for sexual imagery, conversations, and information	Early adolescence
Skill seven	The individual demonstrates functional and effective protest to unwanted or inappropriate solicitations for sexual imagery, conversations, and information	Early adolescence
Teaching format	DTT, Cool versus Not Cool	
Special considerations	Privacy needs can change over time so this should be addressed on an ongoing basis. External privacy controls (e.g., internet blockers) can be used when needed to help ensure individual safety, but should not be used in place of teaching skills. It is sometimes the tendency of those providing sex education to lean too heavily on external controls in place of teaching safety skills. While this may be beneficial until skills are mastered, the need to provide least restrictive environments, respect the individual's right to autonomy, and personal habilitation means that teaching skills related to privacy and safety must be prioritized	

Social interactions

Skill one	The individual connects with known peers in games/apps including sharing contact information (i.e., username)	Early adolescence
Skill two	The individual uses appropriate language in online chat forums (e.g., meets language level used in group, matches teasing level, uses similar tone and slang, etc.)	Early adolescence
Skill three	The individual refrains from bullying when participating in online forums	Early adolescence
Skill four	The individual selects appropriate apps, social media, and games that reflect their own interest and comfort	Adolescence
Skill five	The individual initiates and responds to online flirting behavior (e.g., photos) from known individuals as desired and appropriate. This includes selection of photos that may be flirty or risqué without being pornographic or incongruent with the situation	Adolescence
Skill six	The individual initiates and responds to online flirting behavior (verbal) from known individuals as appropriate and desired. This includes flirting messages that match the situation	Adolescence
Teaching format	DTT, Cool vs. Not Cool, TIP, BST	
Special considerations	It is important that the frame of reference for social interactions in online forums matches that of peers that use the same forum, as such targets should be drawn from this peer environment (i.e., not adult assumptions of appropriate social behavior).	

Online navigation

Skill one	The individual creates, uses, and safely stores appropriate usernames and passwords for online accounts	Early adolescence
Skill two	The individual independently accesses and uses email	Early adolescence
Skill three	The individual proficiently and safely uses age-appropriate social media	Early adolescence
Skill four	The individual proficiently and safely uses age-appropriate online games	Early adolescence
Skill five	The individual demonstrates an understanding of the various privacy and sharing settings on each app/site they use	Adolescence
Skill six	The individual demonstrates an understanding of navigation within various apps (e.g., swiping to respond, etc.)	Adolescence
Skill seven	The individual demonstrates an understanding of the risks of downloading from various sites (e.g., costs, virus risk, distribution of personal information)	Adolescence
Teaching format	DTT, Cool versus Not Cool	

CHAPTER 11

Sexual acts

Abstract

This domain covers sexual acts. An understanding of sexual acts and the formal and casual language used to describe them is important, even if the individual has not demonstrated interest in the particular act. Understanding vocabulary is important as it pertains to the ability to give consent, and safety skills. Additionally, sexual acts may be discussed in nonsexual social situations, observed in TV, movies, and other media, or otherwise shared with the individual learner. Understanding the terminology and scope of the acts is a vital component to these situations. Finally, an understanding of various sexual acts will help inform an individual of their own interest (or disinterest) in engaging in them, leading to overall satisfaction within their own sexual life. As with masturbation, these skills should be targeted in consultation with the learner and the learner's family to ensure congruence with individual and family values and beliefs.

Keywords: Autism; Consent; Oral sex; Sexual acts; Sexual intercourse; Sexual Slang.

Overall goal	• The individual demonstrates an understanding of the following sexual acts: sexual intercourse, anal sex, oral sex • The individual can demonstrate an understanding and usage of common slang terms for sexual intercourse, anal sex, oral sex, and any others relevant to their setting, culture, and social situations
Teaching methodologies	Discrete Trial Teaching, Video Modeling, Parent Coaching
Cross-referenced	Body parts, preferences, abuse prevention and reporting
Special considerations	Even if individuals have not expressed an interest in engaging in any of these sexual acts, it is important for them to be able to recognize these acts as both a safety and social skill. Additionally similarly to social skills and body parts, the selection of slang should be based on same-age and same-community peer input. It is essential that such skills are taught as a continuum of acts that they or others may elect to experience or to not experience. Issues of consent and assent should be embedded into every teaching context.

Clinician's Guide to Sexuality and Autism
ISBN 978-0-323-95743-4
https://doi.org/10.1016/B978-0-323-95743-4.00006-0

An understanding of sexual acts, as well as the formal and casual language used in their discussion is important, even when an individual has not demonstrated an interest in a particular act. Understanding vernacular around sexual acts is a safety skill and helps ensure an understanding of what is being discussed, suggested, or offered. Sometimes it is thought that discussing a sexual act will evoke an interest in that act. It is unlikely that this is what will happen, but is more likely to function to help keep that individual safe.

Additionally, there are many social situations that include demonstrations of sexual acts, or language and innuendo surrounding them. Watching TV or movies, listening to music and others often includes sexual innuendo and not understanding this might hinder one's understanding of the social interactions surrounding such situations. Not understanding the context of the show, etc., may limit one's ability to participate in the social situation surrounding it.

Understanding sexual acts is important if learners are to make informed decisions about whether they they are, or might be, interested in, that particular act. It is important to understand different sexual acts in order to be able to discuss them with partners. Understanding and using vocabulary that goes with particular sexual acts means that individuals can report these to appropriate persons if needed in acts of abuse.

As with other domains that include discussion of vocabulary, it is important that individuals are taught all words that might be used to refer to sexual acts. This includes formal names for acts to be used in discussion with doctors, caregivers, other trusted adults, but also casual terminology or slang that may be used with peers, on media outlets, and with sexual partners. Ensuring that these are taught with a degree of stimulus equivalence will help make sure this is understood. Selection of slang to be targeted should be drawn from the individual's immediate social and peer community.

Sexual acts are an area of teaching that should be approached with sensitivity. Consultation with family is important to ensure targets are congruent with individual and family values and beliefs. Additionally, issues of consent and assent should be emphasized in all aspects of teaching in this domain. Consent and assent are incredibly important in all parts of sexuality, and every opportunity to emphasize it should be taken.

This domain can be taught using Discrete Trial Teaching, Video Modeling, and Parent Coaching. These teaching strategies are outlined in Chapter 3 and should be implemented with individualization to each learner. Not all skills are appropriate to observe in-situ or by video, some are more appropriate to description only. Please use discretion and adjust per your learner. Be aware of laws surrounding depiction of sexual acts in video and picture, and that many of these fall into the category of pornography and should not be used as a teaching tool. Video models are only applicable to early sexual acts.

By school age individuals should be learning to:

- Recognize in pictures, video, and in-situ, and describe the following interactions:
    - o Hugging
    - o Kissing on the cheek
    - o Quick kissing on the lips
    - o Cuddling
    - o Holding hands
- Recognize in pictures, in video, in situ and describe (where appropriate)
    - o Kissing with tongue
    - o Over clothes touching of buttocks, breasts, genitals
- Label and describe the following interactions using proper terminology:
    - o Hugging
    - o Kissing on the cheek
    - o Quick kissing on the lips
    - o Cuddling
    - o Holding hands
- Label and describe the following interactions using slang (if applicable)
    - o Hugging
    - o Kissing on the cheek
    - o Quick kissing on the lips
    - o Cuddling
    - o Holding hands
- Label and describe the following interactions using proper terminology:
    - o Kissing with tongue
    - o Over clothes touching of buttocks, breasts, genitals
- Label and describe the following interactions using slang (if applicable)
    - o Kissing with tongue
    - o Over clothes touching of buttocks, breasts, genitals

By early adolescence individuals should be learning to:

- Recognize in pictures, in video, in situ, and describe (where appropriate):
    - o Undressing another person
    - o Under clothes touching of buttocks, breasts, genitals
    - o Oral sex acts (to a male)
    - o Oral sex acts (to a female)

  - o Vaginal penetration by finger
  - o Vaginal penetration by penis
  - o Vaginal penetration by other object (sex toy)
  - o Anal penetration by finger
  - o Anal penetration by penis
  - o Anal penetration by other object (sex toy)
  - o Masturbation
- Label and describe the following interactions using proper terminology:
  - o Undressing another person
  - o Under clothes touching of buttocks, breasts, genitals
  - o Oral sex acts (to a male)
  - o Oral sex acts (to a female)
  - o Vaginal penetration by finger
  - o Vaginal penetration by penis
  - o Vaginal penetration by other object (sex toy)
  - o Anal penetration by finger
  - o Anal penetration by penis
  - o Anal penetration by other object (sex toy)
  - o Masturbation
- Label and describe the following interactions using slang if applicable:
  - o Undressing another person
  - o Under clothes touching of buttocks, breasts, genitals
  - o Oral sex acts (to a male)
  - o Oral sex acts (to a female)
  - o Vaginal penetration by finger
  - o Vaginal penetration by penis
  - o Vaginal penetration by other object (sex toy)
  - o Anal penetration by finger
  - o Anal penetration by penis
  - o Anal penetration by other object (sex toy)
  - o Masturbation

By adolescence the individual should be learning to:

- Demonstrate an understanding of the existence of various sexual acts including:
  - o Fetish
  - o Multiple partner sex acts
  - o Role-play and dress up
  - o Other relevant preferences
- Use appropriate terminology with appropriate audiences/settings

Sexual acts

Skill one	The individual can recognize in pictures, in video, and in situ, and describe the following interactions: - Hugging - Kissing on the cheek - Quick kissing on the lips - Cuddling - Holding hands	School age
Skill two	The individual can recognize in pictures, in video, in situ, and describe (where appropriate): - Kissing with tongue - Over clothes touching of buttocks, breasts, genitals	School age
Skill three	The individual can recognize in pictures, in video, in situ, and describe (where appropriate): - Undressing another person - Under clothes touching of buttocks, breasts, genitals - Oral sex acts (to a male) - Oral sex acts (to a female) - Vaginal penetration by finger - Vaginal penetration by penis - Vaginal penetration by other object (sex toy) - Anal penetration by finger - Anal penetration by penis - Anal penetration by other object (sex toy) - Masturbation	Early adolescence
Skill four	Demonstrates an understanding of the existence of various sexual acts including: - Fetish - Multiple partner sex acts - Role-play and dress up—other relevant preferences	Adolescence
Teaching format	Parent coaching, DTT	
Special considerations	Not all skills are appropriate to observe in-situ or by video, some are more appropriate to description only. Please use discretion and adjust per your learner. Be aware of laws surrounding depiction of sexual acts in video and picture, and that many of these fall into the category of pornography and should not be used as a teaching tool. Video models are only applicable to early sexual acts. Also consider issues of safety and victimization in all discussions.	

Vocabulary

Skill one	The individual can label and describe the following interactions using proper terminology: - Hugging - Kissing on the cheek - Quick kissing on the lips - Cuddling - Holding hands	School age
Skill two	The individual can label and describe using slang (if applicable) the following interactions: - Hugging - Kissing on the cheek - Quick kissing on the lips - Cuddling - Holding hands	School age
Skill three	The individual can label and describe the following interactions using proper terminology: - Kissing with tongue - Over clothes touching of buttocks, breasts, genitals	School age
Skill four	The individual can label and describe the following interactions (if applicable) using slang terminology: - Kissing with tongue - Over clothes touching of buttocks, breasts, genitals	School age
Skill five	The individual can label and describe the following interactions using proper terminology - Undressing another person - Under clothes touching of buttocks, breasts, genitals - Oral sex acts (to a male) - Oral sex acts (to a female) - Vaginal penetration by finger - Vaginal penetration by penis - Vaginal penetration by other object (sex toy) - Anal penetration by finger - Anal penetration by penis - Anal penetration by other object (sex toy) - Masturbation	Early adolescence

(*Continued*)

Skill six	The individual can label and describe the following interactions (if applicable) using slang terminology - Undressing another person - Under clothes touching of buttocks, breasts, genitals - Oral sex acts (to a male) - Oral sex acts (to a female) - Vaginal penetration by finger - Vaginal penetration by penis - Vaginal penetration by other object (sex toy) - Anal penetration by finger - Anal penetration by penis - Anal penetration by other object (sex toy) - Masturbation	Early adolescence
Skill seven	The individual uses appropriate terminology with appropriate audiences/in appropriate settings	Adolescence
Teaching format	Parent coaching, DTT, TIP, BST	
Special considerations	Age and situation-appropriate slang changes and will vary based on culture and social situations. Make sure that the informants for slang choices are within the population that the learner will use the slang (i.e., ask teenagers what teenagers say, don't try to guess). Different acts may have more than one appropriate slang word—teach as many as currently appropriate.	

CHAPTER 12

Consent

Abstract

Skills in this domain are related to how to provide or obtain consent and assent in a variety of overt and covert sexual situations. Additionally, this domain covers skills related to appropriately responding when consent and assent are given, and when withdrawn. This domain also contains skills related to understanding of breaches of consent as abuse and appropriate steps. This domain is so important. Demonstration of, and recognition of, consent and assent in others is a skill that relies both on vocal communication as well as nonverbal cues, which may be challenging for learners on the autism spectrum. Teaching these skills early and often is vital.

Keywords: Assent; Autism spectrum; Consent; Nonverbal cues; Sexual behavior.

Overall goal	• The individual can demonstrate an understanding of consent and assent as a form of permission to engage, or participate in, a variety of overt and covert sexual situations • The individual can demonstrate consent and assent to sexual acts broadly, in isolation, and under identified circumstances. • The individual can recognize and respond appropriately to consent and assent, or lack thereof, given by another individual • The individual can discern and respond appropriately to situations where a partner has denied consent or assent. • The individual can describe breaches of consent as abuse and follow appropriate reporting
Teaching methodologies	Discrete Trial Teaching, Cool vs. Not Cool, Teaching Interaction Procedure, Behavior Skills Training, Video Modeling
Cross referenced skills	This area overlaps significantly with abuse identification, prevention and reporting, as well as understanding of the law.
Special considerations	This area is challenging to teach within and especially important for both safety concerns and relationships. Discussions must take place in the context of assent/consent and victimization.

Clinician's Guide to Sexuality and Autism
ISBN 978-0-323-95743-4
https://doi.org/10.1016/B978-0-323-95743-4.00013-8

Chapter 1 outlines some of the risks for people on the autism spectrum as pertaining to a need sexuality education. Skills related to effectively giving consent when desired as well as withholding consent when needed are both incredibly important, and may be particularly challenging for people on the autism spectrum. Effectively communicating desires is important, and this requires both recognition of one's own likes and dislikes, as well as effective communication of these. For some people with ASD, they may never have been allowed to refuse a physical greeting, or taught how to. If one is going to be able to give consent, they must first be able to recognize and discuss actions, items, and interactions that they like and do not like. They must have opportunity to practice giving and withdrawing consent and assent in various situations, as well as refusing to give consent at all. Historically, teaching about assent and honoring signs of assent from individuals with ASD has been inexcusably underemphasized. Effectively and confidently giving and withdrawing assent is extremely important in preventing victimization, especially within sexual interactions.

Equally importantly, individuals must be able to recognize both overt and subtle signs of giving and withdrawal of consent by others. While some indices of consent and assent are loud, overt, and clear, others are subtle and rely on interpretation of body language, tone of voice, and other nonverbal cues. A pull away, a pause before saying "yes," and a questioning tone in a vocal agreement can all indicate a withdrawal of assent in an interaction and must be honored as such. For people on the autism spectrum, such cues, especially those that are at all nuanced, may be difficult to interpret correctly, or sometimes to even notice at all. It becomes incredibly important to teach these overtly and to a high degree of fluency.

Skills in the consent domain are closely related to those in both "abuse prevention and reporting" and the law. The overlap is intentional as these skills are of paramount importance for those with ASD.

Skills in the consent domain can be taught using a variety of teaching methodologies including Discrete Trial Teaching, Cool versus Not Cool, Teaching Interaction Procedure, Behavioral Skills Training, and Video Modeling. All teaching strategies are outlined in Chapter 3 and as always should be selected and individualized based on the learner.

Throughout this chapter, we use the terms "primary sexual experiences" and "early sexual experiences" to denote the types of interactions or experiences one might have early in relationships—holding hands, kisses, hugs, and cuddles. It is important that the skills listed above apply to these early experiences as well as those that are more complex. As well it is important to teach giving and recognizing consent and withdrawal in overt ways as well as more subtle behaviors.

Finally, when teaching about consent, the transient or momentary nature of consent should be considered. Consenting to something that someone wants applies in that moment only, and they may change their mind at a later time. This can be a challenging concept for people with ASD, who may have interests that are more rigid and stable, and thus is important to be emphasized within teaching as well.

By preschool age individuals should be learning to:

- Clearly accept physical contact from others (like hugs from family members).
- Identify and clearly protest any unwanted physical contact from others.

By school age, individuals should be learning to:

- Ask before physically engaging with someone in casual physical contact (e.g., a hug) and refrain from engaging in it if the person says no.
- Ask before physically helping someone and refrain from helping if the person says no
- Answer yes/no questions about items/activities they like (e.g., "do you like juice? Do you like roller coasters?")
- Answer yes/no to offers of physical help
- Assert independence by refusing offers or attempts to provide physical help.
- Tell others "I don't like that" and/or move away in response to unwanted physical contact in casual interactions (e.g., someone standing too close, pulling their arm to go somewhere, etc.)
- Answer yes or no to requests for casual physical contact from others (e.g., "can I sit next to you?")

By early adolescence, individuals should be learning to:

- Ask overt questions before physical engaging with others in primary sexual behavior (e.g., "can I hold your hand?")
- Recognize positive or negative body language toward primary sexual behavior and terminate the sexual behavior in response to negative body language from their partner (e.g., turning their face away from a kiss)
- Ask partners what type of primary sexual behavior they like, do not like, or are interested in and they refrain for persistently asking their partner to engage in behaviors their partner has said they do not like
- Ask overt questions before physically engaging with others in all sexual behavior (e.g., "can I kiss you?")

- Recognize positive or negative body language toward all sexual behavior and terminate the behavior in response to negative body language
- Clarify consent for a partner if they are unsure whether consent or assent has been provided.
- Answer yes or no to overt requests for physical contact associated with primary sexual behavior (e.g., can I hold your hand?)
- Nonvocal-verbally agree to primary sexual behavior or can move away from unwanted behavior (e.g., holding the hand of someone who reached for theirs)
- Identify early sexual experiences that they liked, did not like, or are not sure about
- Knowledgeably answer yes or no to overt requests for physical contact for all sexual experiences.

By adolescence, individuals should be learning to:

- Talk about sexual acts with their partner or potential partner in terms of things they like, do not like, and might like to try but have not experienced yet in advance of these happening with a partner
- Tell a partner about aspects of a sexual act they enjoy and the parts they did not enjoy prior to engaging in it, during the act, or following the act
- Demonstrate understanding of when sexual acts have occurred without their consent; recognize this as an act of abuse and behave accordingly.

Demonstrating consent

Skill one	The individual can clearly accept physical contact from others (e.g., hugs from family)	Preschool
Skill two	The individual can identify and clearly protest unwanted physical contact from others	Preschool
Skill three	The individual answers yes or no to questions about items/activities they like (e.g., do you like roller coasters? Juice? etc.)	School age
Skill four	The individual can answer "yes" or "no" to offers of physical help	School age
Skill five	The individual can tell others "I don't like that" and/or move away in response to unwanted physical contact in casual interactions (e.g., someone standing too close, pulling their arm to go somewhere, etc.)	School age
Skill six	The individual can answer "yes" or "no" to requests for casual physical contact from others (e.g., can I shake your hand? Give you a hug? Sit next to you? etc.)	School age
Skill seven	The individual can assert independence by refusing offers of, or attempts to provide, physical help (e.g., someone attempting to adjust their clothing, etc.)	School age
Skill eight	The individual can answer yes or no to overt requests for physical contact associated with primary sexual behavior (e.g., can I hold your hand? Kiss you? Hug you? etc.)	Early adolescence
Skill nine	The individual can nonvocal-verbally agree to primary sexual behavior or can move away from unwanted behavior (e.g., holding hand of someone who reached for theirs, kissing back, etc.)	Early adolescence
Skill ten	The individual can identify early sexual experiences that they liked, did not like, and are not sure about	Early adolescence

(*Continued*)

Skill eleven	The individual can knowledgeably answer yes or no to overt requests for physical contact for all sexual behavior	Early adolescence
Skill twelve	The individual can identify early sexual experiences they liked, did not like, or are undecided about	Early adolescence
Skill thirteen	The individual can talk about sexual acts with their partner or potential partner in terms of things they like, do not like, and might like to try but have not experienced yet in advance of these happening with a partner	Adolescence
Skill fourteen	The individual can tell a partner the aspects of a sexual act that they enjoy and the parts that they do not enjoy either prior to engaging in the act, during the act, or follow the act occurring.	Adolescence
Skill fifteen	The individual demonstrates understanding of when sexual acts have occurred without their consent, recognizes this as an act of abuse, and behaves accordingly (see abuse prevention and recording)	Adolescence
Teaching format	Parent Coaching, DTT, BST/TIP, Cool not Cool	
Special Considerations	There is much overlap in the skills in this domain with many in sexual abuse prevention and reporting, as well as several within social skills. Please ensure complementary skills are being taught together.	

Consent and assent recognition

Skill one	The individual asks before physically engaging with someone in casual physical contact (e.g., can I give you a hug?) and refrains from engaging if the person says "No."	School age
Skill two	The individual asks before physically helping someone and refrains from helping if the person says no	School age
Skill three	The individual asks overt questions before physically engaging with others in primary sexual behavior (e.g., "can I hold your hand?")	Early adolescence
Skill four	The individual recognizes positive or negative body language toward primary sexual behavior and terminates the sexual behavior in response to negative body language from their partner (e.g., turning face away from a kiss, letting go of their hand, etc.)	Early adolescence
Skill five	The individual can ask partners about what types of primary sexual behavior that they like, do not like, or are interested in and refrains from persistently asking their partner to engage in behaviors that their partner has said they do not like	Early adolescence
Skill six	The individual asks overt questions before physically engaging with others in all sexual behavior (e.g., Can I kiss you?)	Early adolescence
Skill seven	The individual recognizes positive or negative body language toward all sexual behavior and terminates the behavior in response to negative body language (i.e., turning face away from a kiss, letting go of their hand, etc.)	Early adolescence
Skill eight	The individual clarifies consent from a partner if the individual is unsure whether consent or assent has been provided.	Early adolescence
Teaching format	Parent Coaching, DTT, BST, TIP, Cool not Cool	

CHAPTER 13

Social skills

Abstract

This domain covers social skills that are particularly applicable to sexuality. Social skills are an integral part of the human experience and as such are complex and may require specified teaching. This is not an exhaustive list of social skills, rather those that are especially relevant in the area of sexuality. Social skills are often specific to the immediate social environment and community and as such these need to be carefully considered. There is strong overlap between this domain and that of relationships as well as individual preference.

Keywords: Autism; Behavior; Compliments; Relationships; Sexuality; Social skills.

Clinician's Guide to Sexuality and Autism
ISBN 978-0-323-95743-4
https://doi.org/10.1016/B978-0-323-95743-4.00012-6

Overall goal	Social skills: • The individual can distinguish between types of relationships by description and in their own life including acquaintances, friends, romantic relationships, and sexual relationships • The individual can distinguish between flirting, teasing, stalking, and bullying • The individual initiates appropriately as desired and responds appropriately to various types of physical interactions (hugging, kissing, sexual acts, etc.) (see consent) • The individual can communicate physical "triggers" to physical or emotional discomfort that need to be avoided • The individual can make social plans that both parties enjoy and follow through with social plans. • The individual can compromise within reason on all parts of a social relationship
Teaching methodologies	Discrete Trial Teaching, Cool vs. Not Cool, Behavioral Skills Training, Teaching Interaction Procedure, Video Modeling
Cross-referenced skills	This area closely aligns with relationships and preferences
Special considerations	Social skills are often highly specific to the immediate social environment/community. Skills like slang, social media use, places people hang out, social activities peer groups engage in, etc., tend to vary from community to community. As such, the social skills targeted as those that reflect the community in which they will be used. Whenever possible, consider using peers to determine what skills should be taught and in what order.

Social skills are complex and are relevant across all aspects of an individual's life. While this domain will only cover those that are directly relevant to sexuality, there is significant overlap between these and social skills that apply to other parts of an individual's life.

The desire for social interaction is variable across people, and sometimes clinicians make the mistake of waiting for an individual to demonstrate particular social interest to begin teaching social skills. This is a mistake, as it discounts the need to have social skills in order to access many of these social environments. The social skills covered in this domain are necessary for comfortable, positive sexual relationships.

Social skills are often highly specific to the immediate social environment/community. Skills like particular slang used, types and amount of social media use, places people hang out, social activities peer groups engage in, etc., tend to vary from community to community. As such, the social skills targeted to be taught should be those that reflect the community in which they will be used. Whenever possible, consider using peers to determine what skills should be taught and in what order.

This domain is closely related to types of relationships and these should be taught in conjunction with each other. Socials skills are interactive, meaning what the learner is expected or required to do is often in response to someone else's social behavior, which may vary greatly across people. Teaching loosely and using a lot of examples will help ensure demonstration of the skills when needed.

Distinguishing between types of interactions as positive (joking, flirting) and negative (bullying) can sometimes be challenging and should be targeted in this area. As well, social interactions require a careful balance of both compromise so that friends and partners get to have plans and activities that they enjoy, as well as standing up for oneself.

There is literature and research available on teaching social skills and individualization of teaching should be utilized with all learners. Social skills can be taught using Discrete Trial Teaching, Cool versus Not Cool, Behavioral Skills Training, Teaching Interaction Procedure, and Video Modeling. See Chapter 3 for further description of these procedures.

By school age individuals should be learning to:

- The individual can determine between "mean" and "nice" things to say to other same-age peers
- Determines "nice" and "mean" things same age peers say
- Recognize and describe interactions that do not include themselves (i.e., people giving compliments, playful teasing, mean teasing)
- Demonstrate use of compliments playful teasing, and mean teasing in various situations
- Recognize when directed to them by others compliments [playful teasing, mean teasing]
- Respond to compliments and playful teasing either reciprocally (giving a compliment or teasing back) ort in another way that is matched to the interaction (e.g., saying "thank you" to a compliment)
- Recognize mean teasing as an act of bullying and can respond by alerting a parent or teacher.
- Initiate greetings with others

- Initiate friendly interactions, questions, or conversations with preferred others
- Initiate requests to add someone new on some variety of social media (both in person and by e-request within the app/system)
- Initiates requests to spend time with others outside of their usual social settings (i.e., hang out outside of school)
- Respond appropriately to greetings from others
- Respond to friendly comments, questions, or conversations as desired
- Respond to requests for adding someone else on carious social media (both in person and within the app/system)
- Responds appropriately to requests to spend time with others outside of the usual setting (i.e., hang out outside of school)
- Communicate to others things they like and dislike when referring to concrete objects, i.e., flavors of chips, types of candy
- Recognize when others communicate preferences that are different than their own
- Respond respectfully to preferences of others that are different from their own (refrains from making disparaging comments about others' preferences)

By early adolescence, individuals should be learning to:

- Initiate requests to exchange contact information with others
- Plan time with others including location, activity, time, transportation
- Respond to requests to exchange contact information with safe others
- Accept invitations to plans made by others
- Exchange contact information with friends/peers including online gaming contacts, phone number, social media contact, and email address
- Store contact information safely
- Not share other people's contact information unless requested or permitted by that person
- Advocate for their own interests and preferences when making plans with others
- Acknowledge and consider the interests and preferences of others when making plans
- Communicate to others things they like and dislike in terms of less concrete items and activities (i.e., types of music, activities, TV shows)
- Consider known information about peer's like and dislikes when making plans (e.g., brings peer's preferred snack)
- Advocate for their own preference when making plans with peers

By adolescence, individuals should be learning to:

- Recognize flirting when seen in interactions that do not involve them (i.e., people in public, TV shows)
- Differentiate physical acts as friendly or sexual in nature even when they are acts that share topography with friendly ones (types of hugs, kiss on the cheek)
- Demonstrate appropriate responses when someone is flirting with them and when the person doing the flirting is a preferred person (i.e., flirting back, smiling)
- Can demonstrate appropriate responses when someone is flirting with them and they want them to stop (i.e., telling them to stop, walking away)
- Initiate appropriate flirting when interested in someone
- Recognize when the person with whom they are flirting wants them to stop and they stop
- Demonstrate an understanding of stalking and recognize when someone is engaging in stalking behavior directed toward them and knows the most appropriate steps to take
- Demonstrates a recognitions of when he or she is engaging in stalking behavior and stops stalking either on their own or when asked
- Organize and make plans with others
- When necessary, cancel plans in a respectful manner

Type of interactions

Skill one	The individual can determine between "mean" and "nice" things to say to other same-age peers	School age
Skill two	The individual can determine "nice" and "mean" things that same age peers say to them	School age
Skill three	The individual can recognize and describe interactions that do not include themselves, i.e., people giving compliments, playful teasing, and mean teasing/making fun of	School age
Skill four	The individual can demonstrate use of compliments, playful teasing, and mean teasing in various situations	School age
Skill five	The individual can recognize when directed to them by others compliments, playful teasing, and mean teasing	School age
Skill six	The individual can respond to compliments and playful teasing either reciprocally (giving a compliment or teasing back), or in another way that is matched to the interaction (i.e., saying "thank you" to a complement)	School age
Skill seven	The individual can recognize mean teasing as an act of bullying and can respond by alerting a parent, teacher, etc.	School age
Skill eight	The individual can recognize flirting when seen in interactions that do not involve them—i.e., people in public, TV shows, etc.	Adolescence
Skill nine	The individual differentiates physical acts as friendly or sexual in nature, even when they are acts that share topography with friendly ones (types of hugs, holding hands, kiss on the cheek, etc.)	Adolescence
Skill ten	The individual can demonstrate appropriate responses when someone is flirting with them and when the person doing the flirting is a preferred person (i.e., flirting back, smiling, etc.)	Adolescence
Skill eleven	The individual can demonstrate appropriate responses when someone is flirting with them and they want them to stop (i.e., telling them to stop, walking away, etc.)	Adolescence

(*Continued*)

Skill twelve	The individual can initiate appropriate flirting when interested in someone.	Adolescence
Skill thirteen	The individual can recognize when the person with whom they are flirting wants them to stop, and they stop	Adolescence
Skill fourteen	The individual demonstrates an understanding of stalking and recognizes when someone is engaging in stalking behavior directed toward them and knows the most appropriate steps to take. (These will vary and may include telling a parent, teacher, or law enforcement personnel based on the severity of the individual's behavior, frequency, past attempts to stop it, etc.)	Adolescence
Skill fifteen	The individual demonstrates a recognition of when he or she is engaged in stalking behavior and stops stalking either on their own or when asked.	Adolescence
Teaching format	Parent coaching, DTT, BST, TIP, Cool not Cool	
Special considerations	There is a significant overlap in the skills in this domain with many in relationships, as well as several within consent. Please ensure complimentary skills are being taught together.	

Initiation of interactions

Skill one	The individual initiates greetings with others	School age
Skill two	The individual initiates friendly interactions, questions, or conversations with preferred others	School age
Skill three	The individual initiates requests to add someone new on some variety of social media (both in person and by e-request within the app/system)	School age
Skill four	The individual initiates requests to spend time with others outside of their usual social setting (i.e., hang out outside of school)	School age
Skill five	The individual initiates requests to exchange contact information with safe others (phone number, email address, etc.)	Early adolescence
Skill six	The individual plans time with others including location, activity, time, transportation, etc.	Early adolescence

Responding to interactions

Skill one	The individual responds appropriately to greetings from others	School age
Skill two	The individual responds to friendly comments, questions, or conversations as desired	School age
Skill three	The individual responds to requests for adding someone else on various social media, (both in person and by e-request within the app/system)	School age
Skill four	The individual responds appropriately to requests to spend time with others outside of the usual setting (i.e., hang out outside of school)	School age
Skill five	The individual responds to requests to exchange contact information with safe others (phone number, email address, etc.)	Early adolescence
Skill six	The individual accepts invitations to plans made by others that include location, activity, times, transportation, etc.	Early adolescence
Teaching format	Parent Coaching, DTT, BST, TIP, Cool not Cool	
Special considerations	There is much overlap in the skills in this domain with many in relationships, as well as several within consent. Please ensure complimentary skills are being taught together.	

Making plans

Skill one	The individual exchanges contact information with friends/peers including online gaming contacts, phone number, social media contact, email address, etc.	Early adolescence
Skill two	The individual stores contact information safely	Early adolescence
Skill three	The individual does not share other people's contact info unless requested or permitted by that person	Early adolescence
Skill four	The individual can advocate for their own interests and preferences when making plans with others	Early adolescence
Skill five	The individual can acknowledge and consider the interests and preferences of others when making plans	Early adolescence
Skill six	The individual can organize and make plans with others	Adolescence
Skill seven	When necessary, the individual cancels plans in a respectful manner	Adolescence
Teaching format	Parent Coaching, DTT, BST/TIP, Cool not Cool	
Special considerations	There is much overlap in the skills in this domain with many in relationships, as well as several within consent. Please ensure complimentary skills are being taught together.	

Communicating preferences

Skill one	The individual can communicate to others things they like and dislike when referring to concrete objects (i.e., flavors of chips, types of candy, games)	School age
Skill two	The individual recognizes when others communicate preferences that are different than their own.	School age
Skill three	The individual responds respectfully to preferences of others that are different than their own (i.e., refrains from making disparaging comments about others' preferences)	School age
Skill four	The individual communicates to others things they like and dislike in terms of less concrete items and activities (e.g., types of music, activities, television shows)	Early adolescence
Skill five	The individual considers known information about peer's likes and dislikes when making plans (e.g., brings the peer's preferred snack)	Early adolescence
Skill six	The individual advocates for their own preferences when making plans with peers	Early adolescence
Teaching format	Parent Coaching, DTT, BST, TIP, Cool not Cool	
Special considerations	There is much overlap in the skills in this domain with many in relationships, as well as several within consent. Please ensure complimentary skills are being taught together.	

CHAPTER 14

Sexual abuse prevention and reporting

Abstract

This domain covers skills related to sexual abuse prevention and reporting. With the unfortunate reality that prevalence of abuse of people with autism spectrum disorders remains disproportionately high, this domain is of the utmost importance. It includes teaching skills related to recognition of acts that are abusive as well as precursors to these acts from both the point of view of the recipient of the act, and the perpetrator of the act. It also includes skills related to evaluating the safety of a situation in advance of being in the situation. One of the most important skills to teach is a functional protest, and several ways to teach this are outlined in this domain.

Finally, while avoiding abusive situations is obviously ideal, it is important that individuals with autism can report unsafe or risky events to a safe person, and accurately recall the events. Skills that cover these areas are included as well.

Keywords: Autism spectrum; Consent; Protest; Self reporting; Sexual abuse; Sexual acts.

Clinician's Guide to Sexuality and Autism
ISBN 978-0-323-95743-4
https://doi.org/10.1016/B978-0-323-95743-4.00005-9

Overall goals	• The individual can recognize acts that are abusive from the point of view of the recipient of the acts • The individual can recognize acts that are potential precursors to abusive acts from the point of view of the recipient of the acts • The individual can recognize acts that are abusive from the point of view of the perpetrator of the acts. • The individual can recognize acts that are potential precursors to abusive acts from the point of view of the perpetrator of the acts • The individual can describe and demonstrate various appropriate strategies for evaluating the safety of a situation in advance of being in the situation • The individual can functionally protest (protest in a way that is effective per situation and makes the listener stop) • The individual can accurately recall events that have transpired • The individual can accurately discriminate events that pose a safety risk • The individual can identify a safe person and share unsafe or risky events that transpired with them
Cross reference	Consent, sexual acts, law, preferences
Teaching methodologies	Discrete Trial Teaching, Cool vs. Not Cool, Teaching Ineteraction Procedure, Behavioral Skills Training
Special considerations	While much of this is written for vocal-verbal communicators, many areas can be adapted to PECS, voice output, or other augmentative users.

Possibly the most terrifying thoughts for parents and caregivers related to sexuality and their children with autism pertain to sexual abuse. This is with good reason. As outlined in Chapter 1, individuals on the autism spectrum are at high risk of victimization, and must be taught skills to help avoid sexually unsafe situations. This is a completely unacceptable situation, and one that requires immediate societal attention and change. It is imperative, however, to also teach skills related to sexual abuse prevention to those on the autism spectrum.

The first steps in abuse prevention are recognizing acts that are abusive, and also recognizing potential precursors to abusive acts. While some determinations about abuse classification are easy to discern, others can be very difficult. For example, sometimes abuse is committed by a trusted adult. Sometimes the victim in an abusive situation doesn't feel unsafe and may even feel special or important. This makes it challenging to recognize in the moment that an act may actually be abusive. As such, when teaching this skill it is important that a focus on what makes an act abusive is prioritized, instead of a focus on the person committing abuse. Abuse can be committed by anyone, including those that are trusted caregivers or others in care positions. We must be careful that we are not teaching people with autism that all caregivers or "close" people are safe, and rather focus on the types of behavior that are appropriate from various people in their life.

Arguably the most important skill that can be taught to people with autism is a functional protest. Functional protest means a protest in the form that it will stop or prevent the undesired action. In some cases, a protest is quiet and polite (e.g., "no thanks" to an offer of food). Other times it must be loud, clear, and forceful as is the case when someone is put in an unsafe situation. Protest should be taught early, across a variety of settings and situations, using a variety of listeners. If we are going to teach people to protest, it means we must also honor their protest and continue to show learners that their protest works.

We also need to teach individuals with autism to evaluate situations for safety before being in the situation, and when a particular situation may become unsafe. Once able to determine the safety or potential risks in a situation we can teach individuals to generate both long- and short-term risk and benefit analyses. These skills will help individuals avoid potentially dangerous situations, and develop skills to help them get out of dangerous situations as they arise.

Finally, while significant efforts should be taken to protect autistic individuals from overtly unsafe situations, they also need to be taught to recall of information and report to correct people. Should an individual with autism be in an unsafe situation, or be a victim of sexual abuse it is extremely important that they are able to report this. This needs to include skills like recalling events up to a prolonged time period passing, determine who is the correct person to share information with, and answer questions related to the information.

As discussed in Chapter 1, not only are people with ASD more likely to be victims of sexual abuse, they are also at risk of committing sexual offenses themselves. This chapter outlines skills related to recognition of acts that are abusive, and precursors to abuse from the perspective of the perpetrator. This will help serve as a safety skill for all parties involved.

This chapter is written with a vocal-verbal learner perspective. With a good understanding of your learner and some creativity, these skills can be adapted well to an augmentative communication user. For example, teaching recall by having a learner take photos on their phone of places they go in a day, people they worked with etc., and use those to answer questions about what they did may be one way to adapt.

Skills in this chapter can be taught using Discrete Trial Teaching, Cool versus Not Cool, Teaching Interaction Procedure, and Behavioral Skills Training. These teaching procedures are outlined in Chapter 3 and as always, should include individualization to the learner.

By preschool age individuals should be learning to:

- Make a choice between a preferred and nonpreferred item
- Protest using a single work to items or activities they do not want
- Say "stop" to ongoing activities they do not want
- Use "no" and "stop" with a variety of adults and peers in various situations
- Recognize by name and description close immediate family members (parent caregiver, siblings, grandparent)
- Demonstrate appropriate interactions with close family members and refrain from them with nonclose family members as desired and appropriate.
- Label current or ongoing physical pain in themselves

By school age individuals should be learning to:

- Protest in advance of an activity (e.g., "I don't want to go there")
- Protest nonpreferred touching by another person under "regular" situations (e.g., I don't want to give that person a hug, I can put on my own sunscreen)
- Protest with follow-up request (I don't want to do that, I want to do this instead)
- Protest using a variety of topographies (i.e., "no!," "no thank you," "STOP," "I don't want to," "leave me alone")
- Adjust their protest to the severity of the situation for themselves (e.g., "no thank you" in response to "Do you want some juice?" vs., "STOP" in response to something more aversive or immediate)
- Protest in a persistent manner (e.g., if the first "stop" didn't result in the person stopping they can repeat it more forcibly)
- Protest using vocabulary and with clear articulation such that they will be understood by their listener.
- Select from an array an item recently (within past 3 min) shown or manipulated.

- Select from an array which item was NOT recently (within past 3 min) shown or manipulated
- Answer questions regarding an even that occurred within that day including questions about people, location, what happened, etc.
- Describe events by generating information regarding setting, people, and other information from events that occurred within that day.
- Answer yes/no and "I don't know" questions about an event they described
- Recognize by name and description extended family members (cousins, aunts/uncles)
- Demonstrate appropriate interactions with extended family members and refrain from them with nonfamily members (i.e., giving hugs) as desired and where appropriate
- Determine what events are noteworthy or out of the ordinary throughout their day (i.e., tell their parents they had a fire drill at school but not that they ate lunch)
- Differentiate between strangers and community helpers.
- Label situations as safe/unsafe when depicted in video and pictures based on their outcomes (e.g., "the ladder was unsafe. I know because the girls fell")
- Label situations as safe/unsafe when depicted in video based on potential for poor outcome (i.e., "the boy COULD fall out of the tree")
- Label current or ongoing physical pain and discomfort in themselves—body part specific if relevant
- Label behavioral indicators of physical pain and discomfort in others.

By early adolescence individuals should be learning to:

- Recall information about an event, item, or activity that occurred within the past 48 h
- Answer questions about an event, item, or activity that occurred within the past 48 h
- Correct another person's incorrect account of an event, item, or activity that occurred within the past 48 h.
- Name or recognize a variety of trusted people in their lives.
- Recognize people in various positions of authority throughout their life and the limits to their authority
- Make fluent in-the-moment decisions and choices about preferred and neutral activities
- Generate possible precautions that could be put in place to minimize safety risk

- Describe the risks and rewards associated with various decisions throughout their life
- Demonstrate behavior that takes appropriate precautions when entering risky situations
- Report physical pain or discomfort that is not ongoing but occurred recently
- Describe and report sources of nonphysical pain or discomfort in themselves (i.e., bullying, harassment)
- Recognize when they are engaging in behavior resulting in nonphysical sources of pain or discomfort for others.

Functional protest

Skill one	The individual can make a choice between a preferred and nonpreferred item	Preschool
Skill two	The individual can protest using single word to items or activities they do not want	Preschool
Skill three	The individual can say "stop" to ongoing activities that they do not want	Preschool
Skill four	The individual can use "no" and "stop" with a variety of adults and peers in various situations	Preschool
Skill five	The individual can protest in advance of an activity (e.g., "I don't want to do that, I don't want to go there")	School age
Skill six	The individual can protest nonpreferred touching by another person under "regular" situations (e.g., I don't want to give that person a hug, I can put on my own sunscreen, etc.)	School age
Skill seven	The individual can protest with follow-up request (e.g., I don't want to do that, I want this instead)	School age
Skill eight	The individual can protest using a variety of topographies (i.e., "no!," "no thank you," "STOP!," "I don't want to," "leave me alone"	School age
Skill nine	The individual can adjust their protest to the severity of the situation for themselves (e.g., "no thank you" in response to "do you want some juice" vs. "STOP!" in response to something more aversive or immediate)	School age
Skill ten	The individual can protest in a persistent manner (e.g., if the first "stop" didn't result in the other person stopping they repeat it more forcefully)	School age
Skill eleven	The individual can protest using vocabulary and with clear articulation such that they will be understood by their listener	School age
Teaching format	Parent Coaching, DTT, BST, TIP, Cool not Cool	
Special considerations	This skill is arguably the most important skill to teach. To be functional, the protest must work for the learner. This skill must be generalized and practiced often, in a variety of settings, with a variety of peers and adults regularly. This section was written for vocal-verbal communicators. For those learners that use an augmentative form of communication, or do not yet have an established form of communication, this is still an incredibly important skill and must be targeted within the individual's current form of communication.	

Recall events

Skill one	The individual can select from an array an item recently (within past 3 min) shown or manipulated	School Age
Skill two	The individual can select from an array which item was NOT recently (within past 3 min) shown or manipulated	School age
Skill three	The individual can answer questions regarding an event that occurred within that day including questions about people, location, what happened, etc.	School age
Skill four	The individual can describe events by generating information regarding setting, people, and other information from events that occurred within that day	School age
Skill five	The individual can answer yes/no and "I don't know" questions about an event they described	School age
Skill six	The individual can recall information about an event, item, or activity that occurred within the past 48 h	Early adolescence
Skill seven	The individual can answer questions about an event, item, or activity that occurred within the past 48 h	Early adolescence
Skill eight	The individual can correct another person's incorrect account of an event, item, or activity that occurred within the past 48 h	Early adolescence
Teaching format	DTT	
Special considerations	Caution needs to be utilized to avoid suggestibility when teaching recall. As well, attention to saliency of events—increased saliency or preference within events may skew objective recall and an aspect of the skill that needs to be considered while teaching	

Discrimination of people and events

Skill one	The individual can recognize by name and description close immediate family members (parent/caregiver, siblings, grandparent)	Preschool
Skill two	The individual can demonstrate appropriate interactions with close family members and refrain from them with nonclose family members (i.e., giving hugs) as desired and appropriate	Preschool
Skill three	The individual can recognize by name and description extended family members (cousins, aunts/uncles)	School age
Skill four	The individual can demonstrate appropriate interactions with extended family members and refrain from them with nonfamily members (i.e., giving hugs) as desired and appropriate	School age
Skill five	The individual can determine what events are noteworthy or out of the ordinary throughout their day (i.e., they tell their parents they had a fire drill at school, not that they ate lunch)	School age
Skill six	The individual can differentiate between friends, acquaintances, and strangers in their life	School age
Skill seven	The individual can differentiate between strangers and community helpers	School age
Skill eight	The individual can name or recognize a variety of trusted people in their lives	Early adolescence
Skill nine	The individual can recognize people in various positions of authority throughout their life, and the limits to their authority	Early adolescence
Teaching format	Parent coaching, DTT, BST, TIP	
Special considerations	Interactions will vary by family rules and cultural values. Additionally, the skills in this area are a moving target—relationships will continue to change over time and this will continually need to be revisited.	

Safety assessment

Skill one	The individual can label situations as safe/unsafe when depicted in video and pictures based on their outcome (e.g., "the ladder was unsafe. I know because the girls fell")	School age
Skill two	The individual can label situations as safe/unsafe when depicted in video and pictures based on potential for poor outcome (e.g., "the boy COULD fall out of the tree")	School age
Skill three	The individual can make fluent in-the-moment decisions and choices about preferred and neutral activities	Early adolescence
Skill four	The individual can generate possible precautions that could be put in place to minimize safety risk	Early adolescence
Skill five	The individual is able to describe the risks and rewards associated with various decisions throughout their life	Early adolescence
Skill six	The individual demonstrates behavior that takes appropriate precautions when entering risky situations	Early adolescence
Special considerations	Assessment of risk is ongoing and changes based on individual circumstance. The learner should be able to use problem-solving and decision-making skills as opposed to learning rote risk assessment.	

Abuse

Skill one	The individual can label current or ongoing physical pain in themselves (not body part–specific)	Preschool
Skill two	The individual can label current or ongoing physical pain and discomfort in themselves— body part–specific if relevant	School age
Skill three	The individual can label behavioral indicators of physical pain and discomfort in others	School age
Skill four	The individual can report physical pain or discomfort that is not ongoing but occurred recently	Early adolescence
Skill five	The individual can describe and report sources of nonphysical pain or discomfort in themselves (i.e., bullying, harassment, etc.)	Early adolescence
Skill six	The individual can recognize when they are engaging in behavior resulting in nonphysical sources of pain or discomfort for others	Early adolescence
Teaching format	Parent consultation, DTT	
Special considerations	For many learners prompting labeling of pain and discomfort in naturally occurring situations may be insufficient frequency for the learner to become fluent in this skill. Care should be taken to contrive teaching opportunities for discomfort where possible.	

CHAPTER 15

Masturbation

Abstract

This domain covers skills related to masturbation. These skills should be targeted with both male and female learners and should be addressed early. It is much easier to teach guidelines around masturbation before they are necessary than to address these skills once masturbation in problematic locations or harmful habits have already developed. These skills should be targeted in consultation with the learner and the learner's family to ensure congruence with family values and beliefs. Care should be taken to teach guidelines for masturbation with long-term application in mind; a bathroom may be a private place in one's home, but is not as private in a public gym changeroom. As such, consideration to discrimination and generalization needs of the learner is important.

Keywords: Autism; Masturbation; Privacy; Sexuality.

Overall goal	• The individual can maintain privacy while masturbating or engaging in genital play. • The individual can masturbate safely and effectively (to orgasm). The individual can masturbate safely and effectively (to orgasm) using lubricant and appropriate aids/toys as necessary • The individual cleans their environment after masturbating including cleaning any aids/toys used, semen, other bodily fluids, etc. • The individual can access legal pornography or other sexual material as desired and can maintain appropriate responsibility of such material (i.e., storing it in a private location)
Teaching methodologies	Discrete Trial Teaching, Video modeling, Cool versus Not Cool, Chaining/Task Analysis Teaching, Parent Coaching
Cross-referenced	Sexual acts, preferences, law
Special considerations	Video modeling can be used when legal and appropriate.

Clinician's Guide to Sexuality and Autism
ISBN 978-0-323-95743-4
https://doi.org/10.1016/B978-0-323-95743-4.00020-5

Masturbation, like other domains, needs to be targeted early. Almost all children will at some point discover touching their genitals, and frankly, that it feels good. As such, there is "built in" reinforcement to this act, and behavior patterns are developed quickly. Teaching the conditions under which masturbation is ok is typically much easier when this is new to learners, and conversely much more challenging to change long-existing behavior patterns. This approach means really consider what the "rule" about masturbation will be that can apply all the time without extra discrimination needed. For example, it might be tempting to teach that a bathroom is a private space and one can masturbate there. And, in some cases a bathroom might be a fully private space (e.g., your bathroom at home). However, a bathroom in a recreation center changing room or public pool is not a private space and engaging in masturbation there is likely to get one in serious trouble. While these distinctions may seem easy to some of us, for people on the autism spectrum distinctions like this can sometimes be challenging. In most cases, it is best to set a conservative rule (e.g., the ONLY place you can masturbate is in your bedroom at home) than try to teach subtleties. Like some other aspects of sexual behavior, the room for error is very small; masturbating in public domains is, in most places, a criminal behavior, the consequences of which can be very serious and long lasting.

There are many other skills that are to be considered within masturbation, including being able to masturbate safely (not using dangerous aids or materials) and effectively (to orgasm). Ineffective masturbation can lead to frustration and challenging behavior. In many cases, effective masturbation is shaped naturally within the act; people continue to do things that feel good. This is also a sensitive and challenging area to teach within and may require the consultation of a sexuality professional should ineffective masturbation become a pervasive problem.

It is also important to teach about hygiene. Masturbation that includes aids or sex toys needs to include instruction on toy storage and cleaning. The individual also needs to learn how to clean themself and any other soiled areas following orgasm.

Access to pornography is also covered in other domains (online activity, law, and individual preference) but the point cannot be overstated. Many individuals that are not of legal age to access pornography are accessing pornography. Many individuals who have parental controls or site locks on their network at home are accessing pornography. The fact is that pornography is accessed, and it is better to teach safe access and management of pornography early and often than to wait until an individual reaches legal age. A discussion of masturbation skills would be remiss to not include this reminder.

Masturbation is challenging to teach. It can be awkward and uncomfortable to talk about, and also deeply personal and private. Masturbation skills can be taught, with discretion, using Discrete Trial Teaching, Cool versus Not Cool, Video modeling, Task Analysis/Chaining, and Parent coaching. These teaching procedures are outlined in Chapter 3. Paying close attention to the people who are teaching these skills and ensuring that they are close, trusted adults, and the pool of teachers in this area is small is important to maintaining safety and privacy.

Finally, autistic learners may often display masturbatory behavior before parents, caregivers, and other adults expect them to do so. Planning ahead and starting early is important to present clear boundaries and conditions under which masturbation is both permitted and safe.

By preschool age, individuals should be learning to:

- Demonstrate an understanding of their own personal private space (typically their bedroom)
- Demonstrate an understanding of their own belongings

By school age, individuals should be learning to:

- Demonstrate an understanding of other people's private space and appropriate rules around this (e.g., knocking on closed door)
- Demonstrate an understanding of other people's belongings and refrain from touching or taking them without permission
- Demonstrate an understanding of the limits of privacy in terms of sound
- Demonstrate an understanding of measures to improve privacy (e.g., playing music to mask sound, closing doors)

By early adolescence, individuals should be learning to:

- Demonstrate respectful behavior of others' privacy including knocking on doors, refraining from searching computer history, and not scrolling through other people's phones
- Identify sex toys/aids and their appropriate use
- Store toys or other masturbation aids (e.g., lubricant) in a safe and private location
- Use toys or other aids in a same manner and refrain from masturbating with necessarily dangerous items (e.g., glass bottles)
- Clean self and any other needed areas following completion

By adolescence, individuals should be learning to:

- Access, manage, and store legal pornography in a safe and private location if applicable
- Regularly check toys for wear and tear, replacing as needed
- Masturbate to orgasm as desired

By adulthood, individuals should be learning to:

- Shop for or otherwise appropriately obtain sex toys, pornography, or other masturbation aids as desired

Privacy

Skill one	The individual demonstrates understanding of their own personal private space (typically their own bedroom)	Preschool
Skill two	The individual demonstrates understanding of their own belongings	Preschool
Skill three	The individual demonstrates understanding of other people's private space and appropriate rules around this—e.g., knocking on the closed door	School aged
Skill four	The individual demonstrates an understanding of other people's belongings and refrains from touching or taking them without permission.	School aged
Skill five	The individual demonstrates an understanding of limits of privacy in terms of sounds	School aged
Skill six	The individual demonstrates an understanding of measures to improve privacy—playing music to mask sound, closing doors, etc.	School aged
Skill seven	The individual demonstrates respectful behavior of others' privacy including knocking on doors, refraining from searching computer history, not scrolling through other people's phones, etc.	Early adolescence
Teaching format	Parent coaching, DTT, Cool versus Not Cool	
Special considerations	Pay close attention to ongoing privacy—many places that appear private (i.e., a public washroom) are still public in terms of masturbation and other sexuality skills. Rules around privacy may be different based on the act being taught—e.g., changing clothes is acceptable in bedroom, public washroom, store changing room, gym lockerroom, etc. Masturbation is only acceptable in one's own bedroom and not the other places listed.	

Toy and material management and hygiene

Skill one	The individual identifies sex toys/aides and their appropriate use	Early adolescence
Skill two	The individual stores toys or other masturbation aids (e.g., lubricant) in a safe and private location	Early adolescence
Skill three	The individual uses toys, or other aides in a safe manner and refrains from masturbating with necessarily dangerous items (e.g., glass bottles)	Early adolescence
Skill four	The individual cleans toys immediately after use	Early adolescence
Skill five	The individual cleans self and any other needed areas following completion (i.e., achieves orgasm)	Early adolescence
Skill six	The individual accesses, manages, and stores legal pornography in a safe and private location	Adolescence
Skill seven	The individual regularly checks toys for wear and tear, replacing as needed	Adolescence
Skill eight	The individual shops for or otherwise appropriately obtains sex toys, pornography, or other masturbation aids.	Adult
Teaching procedures	DTT	
Special considerations	Individuals may require access to masturbation aids before they are able to acquire them themselves. It is important that caregivers are aware of the safety risks of not providing safe aids. Additionally, sex toys can become unsafe over time, or with regular wear and tear. Ideally, an individual is able to learn to discriminate this and replace toys appropriately. If discrimination of this is challenging, an individual may alternately be taught to replace toys on a time-based rotation (i.e., every 12 months).	

Effective masturbation

Skill one	The individual is able to masturbate to orgasm as desired.	Adolescence
Teaching procedures	Task analysis, following a visual schedule	
Special considerations		

CHAPTER 16

Sexual orientation

Abstract

Skills in this area are related to understanding of sexual identity in oneself and others. Formal and slang vocabulary are included, as well as targets related to under what conditions one should use each type of vocabulary and how to recognize and avoid offensive language. This chapter has an additional section on identification of one's own sexual identity, and how and when to communicate that to others.

Keywords: Autism; Bisexual; Gay; Heterosexual; Homosexual; Lesbian; Sexual orientation.

Overall Goal	Sexual orientation: • The individual can recognize their own sexual orientation • The individual can decide if they want to share their sexual orientation and with whom and manage coming out as per their own comfort level • The individual can describe a continuum of sexual orientations and be respectful of those in others • The individual understands, and appropriately uses slang terms related to their own sexual orientation, and can differentiate between acceptable and derogatory slang
Teaching methodologies	Discrete Trial Teaching, Video Modeling, Cool vs. not Cool
Cross-referenced	Gender identity, preferences
Special considerations	For some, sexual orientation is very static throughout their lifetime. For others, this is fluid and may change at different points. As such, some skills may need to be revisited with individuals at later points in time. This is a list of essential, yet discrete, skills and does not address the potential need for individualized emotional support or even therapy when desired by the individual in question.

Clinician's Guide to Sexuality and Autism
ISBN 978-0-323-95743-4
https://doi.org/10.1016/B978-0-323-95743-4.00018-7

Like many aspects of human sexuality sexual orientation is incredibly individualized. For some, their own sexual orientation is simple, straightforward, and static; they may identify consistently with one gender from birth. For others, their orientation may be fluid throughout their lives. While individualized programming is always important, this domain is especially important to tailor to the experiences, feelings, and views of the individual learner.

It is also important to consider that for some learners, working in the domain of sexual identity can be extremely emotionally challenging. It is important to include consultation or collaboration with other professionals to help with emotional support as needed.

This domain can be taught using Discrete Trial Teaching, Video Modeling, Parent Coaching, or Cool versus Not Cool procedures. These teaching procedures are outlined in Chapter 3. As always, teaching procedures should be individualized per learner.

Sexual orientation skills include three main target areas: recognition of sexual orientation in themselves and others, disclosure of their own and others' sexual orientation, and vocabulary related to sexual orientation. All parts are important to teach; however, it is important to realize that this may change over time, and should be revisited regularly.

While we recommend most skills taught in this domain are targeted in early adolescence onwards, if the learner is demonstrating interest or discussion in this area, teaching can begin earlier.

As in other domains teaching about vocabulary is tricky. It is important when teaching slang that the language taught reflects that which will be encountered in the individual's setting. As such, peers, siblings, and other community members should be consulted. As well, in terms of sexual orientation some slang may be derogatory when used under certain conditions but less so under others. These careful discriminations should be taught, as well as skills related to "figuring it out" as new vocabulary is encountered in the future. Similarly good natured teasing often occurs within adolescents and adults. It is important to teach that all slang or derogatory terminology is equivalent, and the ways that some may be more hurtful than others.

Finally, understanding of sexual orientation is a growing area across society. As our understanding of sexuality continues to evolve across time, it is important to ensure that teaching keeps up with societal change.

By early adolescence individuals should be learning to:

- Define and describe various sexual orientations including but not limited to:
  - Heterosexual
  - Homosexual
  - Gay
  - Lesbian
  - Trans
  - Bisexual
  - Asexual
- Demonstrate appropriate understanding when the sexual orientation of someone else is disclosed
- Demonstrate understanding of their own sexual orientation
- Demonstrate understanding that disclosure of sexual orientation is sometimes a private discussion and does not share sexual orientation information about others unless given permission by that person.
- Decide for themselves when to share information about their own sexual orientation
- Decide for themselves with whom to share information about their own sexual orientation
- Share information about their own sexual orientation with appropriate people (e.g., their friends and family, not their teacher at school)
- Demonstrate an understanding of common formal or technical terms related to sexual orientation
- Demonstrate an understanding of common slang terms related to sexual orientation

By now individuals should be learning to:

- Be aware of legislation or regulations that protect their own personal privacy and control of their own disclosure (e.g., employers asking about sexual orientation)
- Recognize potential sources of discrimination related to disclosure of their sexual orientation
- Differentiate between acceptable terms related to sexual orientation and those that are offensive to others
- Refrain from using slang that is discriminatory, derogatory, or otherwise offensive to others

Recognition of sexual orientation

Skill one	The individual defines and describes various sexual orientations including but not limited to heterosexual, homosexual, gay, lesbian, trans, bisexual, and asexual	Early adolescence
Skill two	The individual demonstrates appropriate understanding when the sexual orientation of someone else (family member, friend, acquaintance) is disclosed	Early adolescence
Skill three	The individual demonstrates an understanding of their own sexual orientation	Early adolescence
Teaching format	Parent coaching, DTT	
Special considerations	Recognition of sexual orientation is not the same as appropriate responses to sexual orientation, or other value-based aspects of sexual orientation. These will be addressed within value and preference domains	

Disclosure of sexual orientation

Skill one	The individual demonstrates understanding that disclosure of sexual orientation is sometimes a private decision and does not share sexual orientation information about others unless given permission by that person	Early adolescence
Skill two	The individual decides for themselves when to share information about their own sexual orientation	Early adolescence
Skill three	The individual decides for themselves with whom to share information about their own sexual orientation	Early adolescence
Skill four	The individual shares information about their own sexual orientation with appropriate people (e.g., their friends and family members, not their teacher at school)	Early adolescence
Skill five	The individual is aware of legislation or regulations that protect their personal privacy and control of their own disclosure (e.g., employers asking about sexual orientation)	Adolescence
Skill six	The individual recognizes potential sources of discrimination related to disclosure of their sexual orientation.	Adolescence
Teaching format	Parent coaching, DTT	
Special considerations		

Vocabulary related to sexual orientation

Skill one	The individual demonstrates an understanding of common formal or technical terms related to sexual orientation	Early adolescence
Skill two	The individual demonstrates an understanding of common slang terms related to sexual orientation	Early adolescence
Skill three	The individual differentiates between acceptable terms related to sexual orientation and those that are offensive to others	Adolescence
Skill four	The individual refrains from using slang that is discriminatory, derogatory, or otherwise offensive to others	Adolescence
Teaching procedures	DTT, Cool versus not Cool	
Special considerations	When teaching slang, it is important to consult common uses of slang in the individual's community	

CHAPTER 17

Gender identity

Abstract

Skills in this area are related to an understanding of gender with reference to oneself and/or others. Formal and slang vocabulary are included in teaching, as well as targets related to under what conditions one should use each type of vocabulary and how to recognize and avoid offensive language. An additional section on identification of one's own gender identity, and how and when to communicate that to others is also included.

Keywords: Autism; Binary gender; Gender dysphoria; Gender fluidity; Gender identity; Sexual orientation.

Overall goal	• The individual recognizes and describes their own gender identity • The individual can decide if they want to share their own gender identity and with whom and manage sharing this information as per their own comfort level • The individual can recognize and is respectful of those with other identities including cis and trans • The individual uses pronouns appropriately for self and others
Teaching methodologies	Discrete Trial Teaching, Video Modeling, Cool vs. Not Cool
Cross-referenced	Sexual orientation, preferences
Special considerations	For some, gender identity is very static throughout their lifetime. For others, this is fluid and may change at different points. As such, some skills may need to be revisited with individuals at later points in time. This is a list of essential, yet discrete, skills and does not address the potential need for individualized emotional support or even therapy when desired by the individual in question.

Clinician's Guide to Sexuality and Autism
ISBN 978-0-323-95743-4
https://doi.org/10.1016/B978-0-323-95743-4.00011-4

Like many aspects of human sexuality gender identity is incredibly individualized. For some, their own gender identity is simple, straightforward, and static; they may identify consistently with one gender from birth. For others, gender identity may be fluid throughout their lives. While individualized programming is always important, this domain is especially important to tailor to the experiences, feelings, and views of the individual learner.

It is also important to consider that for some learners, working in the domain of gender identity can be extremely emotionally challenging. It is important to include consultation or collaboration with other professionals to help with emotional support as needed.

This domain can be taught using Discrete Trial Teaching, Video Modeling, Parent Coaching, or Cool versus Not Cool procedures. These teaching procedures are outlined in Chapter 3. As always, teaching procedures should be individualized per learner.

Gender identity skills include three main target areas: recognition of gender identity in themselves and others, disclosure of gender identity, and vocabulary related to gender identity. All parts are important to teach; however, it is important to realize that this may change over time, and should be revisited regularly.

While we recommend most skills taught in this domain are targeted in early adolescence onwards, if the learner is demonstrating interest or discussion in this area, teaching can begin earlier.

As in other domains teaching about vocabulary is often tricky. It is important when teaching slang that the language taught reflects that which will be encountered in the individual's setting. As such, peers, siblings, and other community members should be consulted. As well, in terms of gender identity some slang may be derogatory when used under certain conditions but less so under others. These careful discriminations should be taught, as well as skills related to "figuring it out" as new vocabulary is encountered in the future. Similarly good-natured teasing often occurs within adolescents and adults. It is important to teach that all slang or derogatory terminology is equivalent, and the ways that some may be more hurtful than others.

Finally, understanding of gender identity is a growing area across society. As our understanding of gender continues to evolve across time, it is important to ensure that teaching keeps up with societal change and scientific understanding.

By early adolescence individuals should be learning to:

- Define and describe binary gender identity
- Define and describe gender fluidity, gender nonbinary, and gender dysphoria
- Demonstrate empathy, understanding, or support when the gender orientation of someone else is disclosed
- Demonstrate understanding of their own biological sex and their own gender
- Demonstrate an understanding that the disclosure of gender identity is a private decision and doesn't share information about the gender identity of others without permission
- Decide for themselves with whom to share information about their own gender identity
- Only share information about their own gender identity with appropriate people
- Demonstrate understanding of formal or technical terms related to gender identity
- Demonstrate understanding of common informal or slang terms related to gender identity
- Demonstrate the ability to differentiate between acceptable terms related to gender identity and those offensive to others
- Refrain from using slang that is discriminatory, derogatory, or otherwise offensive to others.

By adolescence individuals should be learning to:

- Be aware of legislation or regulations that protect the personal privacy and control of their own disclosure (e.g., employers cannot ask about sexual orientation or gender identity)
- Recognize potential sources of discrimination related to disclosure of their gender identity
- Recognize when they have been the victim of discrimination and can report this to the correct individual

Recognition of gender identity

Skill one	The individual defines and describes binary gender identity	Early adolescence
Skill two	The individual defines and describes gender fluidity, gender nonbinary, and gender dysphoria	Early adolescence
Skill three	The individual demonstrates empathy, understanding or support when the gender orientation of someone else (family member, friend, acquaintance) is disclosed	Early adolescence
Skill four	The individual demonstrates understanding of their own biological sex and their own gender	Early adolescence
Teaching format	Parent coaching, DTT	
Special considerations	Recognition of gender identity is not the same as appropriate responses to gender identity, or other value-based aspects of gender. These will be addressed within value and preference domains.	

Disclosure of gender identity

Skill one	The individual demonstrates understanding that disclosure of gender identity is generally a personal/private decision, and so does not share information regarding the gender identity of others unless given permission	Early adolescence
Skill two	The individual decides for themselves when to share information about their own gender identity	Early adolescence
Skill three	The individual decides for themselves with whom to share information about their own gender identity	Early adolescence
Skill four	The individual shares information about their own gender identity with appropriate people (e.g., their friends, certain family members but generally not the cashier at the grocery story)	Early adolescence
Skill five	The individual is aware of legislation or regulations that protect their personal privacy and control of their own disclosure (e.g., employers may not ask about sexual orientation, etc.)	Adolescence
Skill six	The individual recognizes potential sources of discrimination related to disclosure of their gender identity	Adolescence
Skill seven	The individual recognizes when they have been the victim of discrimination and can report this to the correct individual	Adolescence
Teaching format	Parent coaching, DTT	
Special considerations		

Vocabulary related to gender identity

Skill one	The individual demonstrates understanding of common formal or technical terms related to gender identity	Early adolescence
Skill two	The individual demonstrates understanding of common informal, or slang terms, related to gender identity	Early adolescence
Skill three	The individual demonstrates the ability to differentiate between acceptable terms related to gender identity and those that are offensive to others and under what conditions	Early adolescence
Skill four	The individual refrains from using slang that is discriminatory, derogatory, or otherwise offensive to others	Early adolescence
Teaching procedures	DTT, Cool versus Not Cool	
Special considerations	When teaching slang, it is important to consult common uses of slang in the individual's community	

CHAPTER 18

Individual preferences

Abstract

This domain covers skills related to individual's preferences in terms of menstrual care products, masturbation aids, sexual intimacy, dating activities, and birth control. The identification of preference, as well as the ability to make and communicate choices related to preferences is greatly important to autonomy, and overall quality of life.

Keywords: Birth control; Dating; Masturbation aids; Menstrual care products; Pornography; STD.

Overall goal	• The individual can recognize their own preferences in the areas of: **o** Menstrual care product **o** Masturbation aids **o** Sexual intimacy **o** Dating activities and settings **o** Birth control • The individual can effectively communicate their choice in the above areas. • The individual can make choices among items in the above areas
Teaching methodologies	Discrete Trial Teaching, Behavioral Skills Training, Teaching Interaction Procedure
Cross-referenced skills	This area closely aligns with social skills
Special considerations	It is important to remember that preferences are individual and change over time. Preferences may change with circumstances, and may vary across individuals (e.g., sexual acts that an individual prefers with one person may be different with another). Continued targeting of these areas over time is recommended.

Clinician's Guide to Sexuality and Autism
ISBN 978-0-323-95743-4
https://doi.org/10.1016/B978-0-323-95743-4.00003-5

Honoring individual preferences is important to everyone. When our choices and options are restricted, it can be extremely frustrating. This is true especially within the realm of sexuality, and equally true for those on the autism spectrum. Having preferences respected and honored is important for autonomy in decisions and overall quality of life.

Preference comes on many levels. When considering, for example, preference for menstrual products one has to have experienced types of products (how do you know if you even like tampons without trying them?). Then within the type of product there is such broad availability of brand, size, and type. These preferences, both broad and specific, are really important to most people. They may be static (I always prefer one brand over another) or may change over time. As such, they are some important considerations when teaching preferences within the realm of sexuality.

The first consideration, which may feel obvious, but is often overlooked when working with individuals with ASD, is that in order for someone to determine whether an item is preferred or not they must be exposed to the item. As such, it is important to ensure we are offering a variety of items; for example, when teaching menstrual care, we need to ensure we are offering different styles, types, and brands of products. Often, we teach skills in sexuality domains without a lot of consideration to these aspects.

Preference also includes being able to effectively communicate preferences to others both spontaneously (as in, "would you like to go to a movie tonight?" or as a choice, "should we go see movie A or movie B?"), and as articulation of the preferred choice and the not preferred one.

When considering preferences, there are complicating factors that play into each area. Sometimes preferences are related to long-term effects, i.e., one brand of birth control pill has fewer side effects than the other. This can be difficult to discern sometimes, and teaching may need to help bring attention to these variables. Additionally, some preferences are idiosyncratic, i.e., some sexual activities are better with some people than others. This means that recognizing and communicating preference can be situational and complicated. Finally, preferences change over time. This means that reviewing preferences often is important.

Teaching about preferences can be done using Discrete Trial Teaching, Behavioral Skills Training, and Teaching Interaction Procedure. See Chapter 3 for more detailed explanations of these teaching procedures, and as always teaching should be individualised per learner.

By school age individuals should be learning to:

- Identify their own likes and dislikes in terms of items and activities (e.g., the types of movies they like to watch, type of food they like)
- Be respectful and acknowledge the preferences of others even if they are different than their own

By early adolescence individuals should be learning to:

- Recognize their preferred masturbation aids (e.g., vibrators, lotion, etc.)
- Make choices between available masturbation aids
- Plan dates that consider their partner's preferences
- Advocate for their own preferences in making plans with partners
- Make considerations to safety and overall comfort when planning for dating activities (i.e., plans to meet new people in public places)
- Recognize that sexual preferences are generally individualized and subjective as they pertain to both self and others (e.g., being a "bad kisser" is related to individual preferences in style, and not an objective assessment of one's ability)

By adolescence individuals should be learning to:

- Try different styles of menstrual products (e.g., pad, tampon) if desired
- Try different brands of menstrual products within regularly used types
- Select preferred or currently desired menstrual product from available choices
- Indicate a preferred or currently desired menstrual care product spontaneously to a known person
- Demonstrate an understanding of the various types of birth control and the risks and benefits associated with each
- Communicate their preference for birth control type with their partner as needed
- Take into consideration their partner's preference for birth control type as appropriate
- Within a type of birth control select their preferred type considering a variety of related factors (e.g., protection against pregnancy, protection against STI/STD, ability to remember to take their pill every day)
- Within a type of birth control demonstrate and communicate preference for brand if applicable
- If unhappy with a type of birth control the individual will communicate their displeasure and reasons why with the appropriate person (e.g., informing doctor of unpleasant side effects)
- Within legal limits the individual recognizes preferred categories of pornography

- Within legal limits the individual requests of otherwise obtains preferred categories of pornography
- When needed or appropriate the individual communicates their preference in pornography to a sexual partner
- The individual recognizes their own enjoyment, pleasure, or discomfort in the moment while engaging in any level of sexual act either verbally (e.g., saying "I like that" or "that's a little too much") or with body language (smiling, leaning in, pulling away)
- Communicate information about sexual acts they have enjoyed or ones they have not enjoyed in the past to current/future partners
- Use past sexual experiences to assess whether they might enjoy something they haven't experienced and communicate this to a partner

Menstrual care

Skill one	The individual tries different styles of menstrual products (e.g., pad, tampon, menstrual cup, period underwear) if desired	Adolescence
Skill two	The individual tries different brands of menstrual products within regularly used types (this is generally advisable to review and practice prior to onset of menstruation)	Adolescence
Skill three	The individual selects preferred or currently desired product from available choices	Adolescence
Skill four	The individual indicates preferred or currently desired product spontaneously to a known person	Adolescence
Teaching format	DTT	
Special considerations	Menstrual care product preference may change based on timing within the individual's cycle, and activities in which the individual is engaging. For individuals who demonstrate a strong preference to type or brand of product, ensuring some flexibility in accepting less preferred items is recommended to ensure acceptance of alternative products in unexpected or uncontrollable circumstances where the most preferred product is unavailable.	

Birth control

Skill one	The individual demonstrates understanding of various types of birth control and the benefits and risks associated with each	Adolescence
Skill two	The individual communicates their preference for birth control type (e.g., birth control pill, condom) with their partner as needed	Adolescence
Skill three	The individual takes into consideration their partner's preference for birth control type as appropriate	Adolescence
Skill four	Within a type of birth control, the individual selects their preferred type, considering a variety of related factors (e.g., protection against pregnancy, protection against STI/STD, ability to remember to take their pill every day)	Adolescence
Skill five	Within a type of birth control the individual demonstrates and communicates preference for brand if applicable.	Adolescence
Skill six	If unhappy with a type of birth control, the individual communicates their displeasure and reasons why with appropriate person (e.g., informing her doctor of uncomfortable side effects of current birth control pill)	Adolescence

Masturbation aids

Skill one	The individual recognizes preferred masturbation aids (e.g., vibrators, lotion, fleshlight)	Early adolescence
Skill two	The individual makes choices between available masturbation aids	Early adolescence
Skill three	The individual spontaneously requests or otherwise obtains (e.g., purchase online, at an adult store, or other vendor) preferred masturbation aids	Early adolescence
Skill four	Within legal limits, the individual recognizes preferred categories of pornography	Adolescence
Skill five	Within legal limits, the individual requests or otherwise obtains preferred categories of pornography	Adolescence
Skill six	When needed or appropriate, the individual communicates their preference in types of pornography to a sexual partner	Adolescence
Teaching format	DTT	
Special considerations	In terms of preferences with pornography, while legal age limits exist to accessing pornography, it is reasonable to assume in many cases that the individual may be accessing pornography before the legal age. It is important to address preferences in pornographic content in terms of legal rules, even with individuals who may not yet meet the legal age to procure pornography. Instruction in what pornography is illegal (e.g., child pornography, "snuff" films) or would generally be considered problematic (e.g., depictions of rape or incest) should be considered essential.	

Dating activities

Skill one	The individual identifies their own likes and dislikes in terms of items and activities (e.g., types of movies they like to watch, food they like)	School age
Skill two	The individual is respectful and acknowledges the preferences of others, even if different than their own	School age
Skill three	The individual plans dates that consider their partner's preferences	Early adolescence
Skill four	The individual advocates for their own preferences in making plans with partners	Early adolescence
Skill five	The individual makes considerations to safety and overall comfort when planning for dating activities (i.e., plans to meet new people in public places, plans for safe transportation to dates)	Early adolescence
Teaching format	Parent coaching, DTT, BST, TIP, Cool not Cool	
Special considerations	There is much overlap here with social skills domains—be sure to cross-reference and target both.	

Sexual acts

Skill one	The individual recognizes and demonstrates an understanding that sexual preferences are generally individualized and subjective as they pertain to both self and others (e.g., being a "bad kisser" is related to individual preferences in style, not an objective assessment of their ability)	Early adolescence
Skill two	The individual recognizes their own enjoyment, pleasure, or discomfort in the moment while engaging in any level of sexual act	Adolescence
Skill three	The individual demonstrates/communicates their own enjoyment or discomfort in the moment while engaging in any level of sexual act either verbally (e.g., saying "I like that" or "that's a little too much"), or with body language (e.g., smiling, leaning into someone pulling away)	Adolescence
Skill four	The individual communicates information about sexual acts they have enjoyed, or ones they have not enjoyed in the past, to current or future partners	Adolescence
Skill five	The individual will use past sexual experiences to assess whether they might enjoy something they haven't experienced and communicate this to a partner	Adolescence
Teaching format	BST, TIP, Cool not Cool	
Special considerations	Careful consideration of teaching strategies is important in this domain. Using parallels to other successful methods in teaching preference may be beneficial. Consider carefully the instructor and the relationship they have with the learner, being mindful of maintaining boundaries of professional relationships. Focus on teaching ways to communicate preferences in sexual acts using BST/TIP	

CHAPTER 19

Types of relationships

Abstract

This domain covers skills related to different types of relationships. It is sometimes challenging to have clear definitions of the type of relationship one finds themselves in, particularly if they desire to be in a different type of relationship. This domain covers skills related to understanding different types of relationships and the behaviors common within them. Skills also include demonstrating understanding of the fluent and transient nature of relationships, and a recognition and management of relationship change.

Keywords: Autism; Consent; Physical interactions; Potential for abuse; Relationship; Trusted adult.

Overall goal	• The individual demonstrates an understanding of various types of relationships as they pertain to themselves and others • The individual demonstrates an understanding of appropriate or expected behavior common in various types of relationships • The individual demonstrates an understanding of fluent or transient nature of relationships, and recognizes signs of relationships changing
Teaching methodologies	Discrete Trial Teaching, Behavioral Skills Training, Teaching Interaction Procedure, Cool vs. Not Cool
Cross-referenced skills	This area closely aligns with social skills, preferences, consent, and abuse prevention
Special considerations	This area is somewhat nuanced; it is important to teach and assess regularly

It can sometimes be difficult to discern what type of relationship one is in with someone else, especially in early days of dating or sexual relationships. Relationships with people change, and can move from friendship to romantic partner and sometimes back again. Each type of

Clinician's Guide to Sexuality and Autism
ISBN 978-0-323-95743-4
https://doi.org/10.1016/B978-0-323-95743-4.00001-1

relationship comes with different expectations and understandings of parameters for how each person should act. These extend to physical interactions, the way that each partner speaks to each other, methods of contact, what type of personal information they share, and what other types of personal interactions can be expected. Some of these relationship types are straightforward, clear, and easy to define. Others however may be more nuanced, fluid, and unclear. These relationships have potential for serious implications if the "rules" of the relationship are not clearly understood by all parties. Potential for abuse, issues related to consent, and even legal issues can arise if the type and parameters of the relationship are not clearly understood.

The changing nature of relationships may be challenging for people with autism to understand, and as such should, early on be the focus of teaching. Interpersonal cues and other ways to understand what type of relationship one is in with a person should be taught, as opposed to teaching that particular people are in specific types of relationships. The exception to this can include close family members (parents, siblings). As types of relationships change over time, these skills should be reviewed regularly.

This area has nuances that vary across individual circumstances. For example, some families are physically close and may cuddle on the couch, hug often, even cosleep. Others may be very physically distant. It is important to ensure that learners are being taught parameters for relationships with consideration to these individualized circumstances.

Skills in this domain can be taught using Discrete Trial Teaching, Behavior Skills Training, Teaching Interaction Procedure, and Cool versus not Cool. See Chapter 3 for a full description of these teaching methods and individualize per learner.

By early adolescence individuals should be learning to:

- Demonstrate understanding of the differences between relationship types including:
  - Close family
  - Extended family
  - Acquaintance
  - Friend
  - Close friend

  - o Peer/classmate
  - o Trusted adult (known)
  - o Trust adult (community person)
  - o Romantic/sexual interest
  - o Romantic/sexual interest—casual
  - o Romantic/sexual interest—serious
  - o Ex-romantic/sexual partner
  - o Any additional types of relationships that might be relevant for that individual's life/culture
- Demonstrate understanding of fluidity—that people may not necessarily be in one type of relationship only (e.g., may move from friend to romantic interest)
- Demonstrate understanding that people may be in different categories of relationship at the same time (e.g., classmate and romantic interest)
- Demonstrate an understanding of expected behavior by people in various types of relationships including:
  - o Physical interactions
  - o Types of language used
  - o Methods of contact
  - o Personal information sharing
  - o Other personal interactions (sharing food, loaning money)
- Demonstrate understanding of how people in various relationships act toward one another. This includes:
  - o Physical interactions
  - o Types of language used
  - o Methods of contact
  - o Personal information sharing
  - o Other personal interactions (sharing food, loaning money)
- Demonstrate an understanding of how they should/can act with others in various types of relationships. This includes:
  - o Physical interactions
  - o Types of language used
  - o Methods of contact
  - o Personal information sharing
  - o Other personal interactions (sharing food, loaning money)

- Demonstrates an understanding of when someone is acting to them in a way that is unexpected or inappropriate for their relationship status including
    - o Physical interactions
    - o Types of language used
    - o Methods of contact
    - o Personal information sharing
    - o Other personal interactions (sharing food, loaning money)
- Communicate with relevant persons if someone is acting in a harmful or dangerous way for their relationship type (e.g., a family member being abusive)

  By adolescence individuals should be learning to:
- Discriminate between relationships based on external factors (e.g., related to family, trusted adult community)
- Discriminate between relationships that exist based on interactions (e.g., a close friend is someone you trust a lot, tell important things to, does nice things for you)
- Describe indicators of a relationship that has moved from one type to another
- Place known and relevant people in their life into various relationship categories.

Types of relationships

Skill one	The individual demonstrates understanding of differences between relationship types including: - Close family - Extended family - Acquaintance - Friend - Close friend - Peer/classmate - Trusted adult (known) - Trusted adult (community person) - Romantic/sexual interest - Romantic/sexual partner—casual - Romantic/sexual partner—serious - Ex-romantic/sexual partner * Any additional types of relationship that may be relevant in that individual's life/culture	Early adolescence
Skill two	The individual demonstrates understanding of fluidity —that people may not necessarily be in one type of relationship only (e.g., may move from friend to romantic interest)	Early adolescence
Skill three	The individual demonstrates understanding that people may be in different categories of relationship at the same time (e.g., classmate and romantic interest)	Early adolescence
Skill four	The individual is able to discriminate between relationships based on external factors (e.g., related to family, trusted adult—community is someone who works in doctor office, etc.)	Adolescence
Skill five	The individual is able to discriminate between relationships that exist based on interactions (e.g., a close friend is someone that you trust a lot, tell important things to, does nice things for you)	Adolescence
Skill six	The individual can describe indicators of a relationship that has moved from one type to another. This will vary based on relevant types of relationships in the individual's life at the time.	Adolescence

(*Continued*)

Skill seven	The individual can place known and relevant people in their life into various relationship categories (i.e., they can identify a their own neighbor as an acquaintance, their aunt as a family member, etc.)	Adolescence
Teaching format	DTT	
Special considerations	Some types of relationships apply more at different parts of someone's life than others. As well, some individual circumstances may apply (e.g., a friend's parent may be a trusted adult, while other friend's parents may be just acquaintances).	

Expectations of relationships

Skill one	The individual demonstrates an understanding of expected behavior by people in various types of relationships including: - Physical interactions - Types of language used - Methods of contact - Personal information sharing - Other personal interactions (sharing items, sharing food, lending money, etc.)	Early adolescence
Skill two	The individual demonstrates an understanding of how people in various relationships act toward one another. This includes: - Physical interactions - Types of language used - Methods of contact - Personal information sharing - Other personal interactions (sharing items, sharing food, lending money, etc.)	Early adolescence
Skill three	The individual demonstrates an understanding of how they should/can act with others in various types of relationships. This includes: - Physical interactions - Types of language used - Methods of contact - Personal information sharing - Other personal interactions (sharing items, sharing food, lending money, etc.)	Early adolescence
Skill four	The individual demonstrates an understanding of when someone is acting to them in a way that is unexpected or inappropriate for their relationship status. This includes: - Physical interactions - Types of language used - Methods of contact - Personal information sharing - Other personal interactions (sharing items, sharing food, lending money, etc.)	Early adolescence

(Continued)

Skill five	The individual communicates with relevant persons if someone is acting in a harmful or dangerous way for their relationship type (e.g., a family member being abusive)	Early adolescence
Teaching format	DTT, BST, TIP, parent coaching, Cool Not Cool	
Special considerations	Some rules of relationships are very clear and nonnegotiable, particularly those relating to legal issues, consent, and potential for abuse. Others however, may vary based on individual circumstances (e.g., some families are physically very close, others are not). Ensure that both broad and individual circumstances are addressed.	

CHAPTER 20

Problem solving and critical thinking

Abstract

This domain covers skills related to problem solving and critical thinking which are important to short-term decision making (i.e., planning where to go on a date), longer-term problem solving (i.e., how to deal with conflict with a partner in a respectful way), and remaining safe (i.e., what should I do if I feel unsafe? Where can I find resources about abuse?). Skills in this domain will cover teaching in-the-moment problem solving, skills related to finding and procuring resources, and planning skills.

Keywords: Autism; In-the-moment decisions; Planning; Problem-solving and critical thinking.

Overall goal	• The individual demonstrates in-the-moment problem solving • The individual demonstrates ability to find resources in various places • The individual demonstrates planning ahead skills within safety and social priorities
Teaching methodologies	Discrete Trial Teaching, Behavioral Skills Training, Teaching Ineteraction Procedure, Cool vs. Not Cool, Parent Coaching
Cross- referenced skills	This area closely aligns with abuse prevention
Special considerations	The goal of this domain is to teach overall problem-solving skills, not simply the solutions to a variety of problems they may encounter. As such, teaching broadly, loosely, and with many exemplars is important.

Problem-solving and critical thinking skills extend far beyond sexuality skills. Problem-solving skills are important in many aspects of life and they have direct implications within sexuality teaching. The goal of this domain is to teach overall problem-solving skills, not simply the solution to

Clinician's Guide to Sexuality and Autism
ISBN 978-0-323-95743-4
https://doi.org/10.1016/B978-0-323-95743-4.00010-2

problems. It is impossible to teach all problematic situations an individual may encounter; behavior and life are complex and the situations individuals encounter across their life are often novel and include complicated maintaining contingencies. While teaching direct skills is important, it is also important to teach individuals skills related to critical thinking.

Critical thinking skills involve both planning ahead, considering possible concerns, variable outcomes, and anticipating "changes in plans." As in other domains, these skills can be targeted in younger children without including sexuality-specific targets. These skills should be developed early, and targeted often. Teach children to plan ahead; consider the situation they will be in, apply their learning of past experiences, and consider alterative plausible needs of future situations. Teach individuals to be responsible for their own materials and possessions; this will help not only with responsibility but also increase awareness of their environment which is an important safety skill.

Critical thinking also includes making quick in-the-moment decisions. Sometimes we have a long time to think out problems, but sometimes situations require a quick decision and being able to make decisions quickly without panicking is important.

Finally, identifying resources for different topics and parts of life is important. Understanding who to ask for what is important, both for getting the accurate answer to your question and, once again, as a safety skill.

Problem-solving and critical thinking skills can be taught using Discrete Trial Teaching, Behavior Skills Training, Teaching Interaction Procedures, and Parent Coaching. Further description of these can be found in Chapter 3. As always, individualization per learner is important. While teaching broadly and loosely and with lots of exemplars is important in all teaching, in this domain this will help lead to acquisition of problem-solving skills, not just an answer to specific questions.

By school age individuals should be learning to:

- Collect and manage their own needed items when leaving for an activity immediately (e.g., getting bathing suit and towel to go swimming; hat and mitts when told its cold out)
- Collect and manage their own items for future events (e.g., packs an overnight bag)
- Find contact information if needed for social plans.
- Recognize possible outcomes or things that could happen next in contrived situations

- Recognize and describe several possible "next step" in the moment (e.g., If my marker isn't working I can ask a teacher for a new one OR use a different color)
- Ask clarifying questions about information presented to them about a variety of topics
- Identify relevant "experts" in their life and their topics (e.g., my friend plays guitar, he might know the answer to this music question)

By early adolescence individuals should be learning to:

- Carry, keep charged, and maintain responsibility for their own phone
- Recognize and discuss potential safety concerns when making plans
- Plan alternative or add safeguards to unsafe situations
- Make excuses or change plans in the moment when needed
- Manage plans being changed with short notice and make decisions about whether to participate
- Discriminate and identify appropriate people to ask questions related to sexuality topics (i.e., a parent may be an appropriate person to ask about menstrual care, but an older sibling may be an appropriate person to ask about online activity)
- Search internet resources safely and with a critical view to accuracy of information

By adolescence individuals should be learning to:

- Have an exit plan for unsafe or uncomfortable situations and can demonstrate (at least in practice)
- List and understand how to access various additional health resources (i.e., school nurse, family doctor, planned parenthood resources)
- Access and use emergency resources if needed

Planning ahead

Skill one	The individual collects and manages their own items needed when leaving for an activity immediately (e.g., "its time to go swimming, get your things"—they collect their bathing suit, towel, etc., or "its cold outside today"—gets hat and mitts)	School age
Skill two	The individual collects and manages own items for future event (e.g., packs overnight bag)	School age
Skill three	The individual finds contact information if needed for social plans (address, phone number of other people)	School age
Skill four	The individual carries, keeps charged, and maintains responsibility for their own phone	Early adolescence
Skill five	The individual recognizes and discusses potential safety concerns when making plans	Early adolescence
Skill six	The individual plans alternatives or adds safeguards to unsafe situations	Early adolescence
Teaching format	Parent coaching, DTT, BST, TIP, Cool not Cool	
Special considerations	There is much overlap here with abuse prevention.	

In-the-moment decisions

Skill one	In contrived situations the individual can recognize possible outcomes or "things that could happen next"	School age
Skill two	In the moment the individual can recognize and describe several possible "next steps" (e.g., if my marker isn't working I can find a teacher and ask for a new one, OR use a different color)	School age
Skill three	The individual can make excuses or change plans in the moment when needed	Early adolescence
Skill four	The individual can manage plans being changed with short notice and make decisions about whether to participate	Early adolescence
Skill five	The individual has an exit plan for unsafe or uncomfortable situations and can demonstrate (at least in practice)	Adolescence
Teaching format	Parent coaching, DTT, BST, TIP, Cool not Cool	
Special considerations		

Resources

Skill one	The individual is able to ask clarifying questions about information presented to them about a variety of topics	School age
Skill two	The individual is able to identify relevant "experts" in their life and their topics (e.g., "my friend plays guitar, he might know the answer to this music question")	School age
Skill three	The individual is able to discriminate and identify appropriate people to ask questions related to sexuality topics (i.e., their parent may be an appropriate person to ask about menstrual care, their older sibling may be an appropriate person to ask about online activity)	Early adolescence
Skill four	The individual can search internet resources safely and with a critical view to accuracy of information	Early adolescence
Skill five	The individual is able to list, and understand how to access various additional health resources (i.e., school nurse, family doctor, planned parenthood resources)	Adolescence
Skill six	The individual is able to access and use (if needed) emergency resources (i.e., help phone numbers)	Adolescence
Teaching format	Parent coaching, DTT, BST, TIP, Cool not Cool	
Special considerations	This area overlaps with relationships and abuse prevention. Resources will vary by areas, it is important to ensure accuracy in available resources for the area in which individuals access services and live.	

Appendix

CHAPTER 21

Resources

Abstract

This chapter includes resources for various components of teaching about sexuality for people on the autism spectrum.

Keywords: Autism; Puberty; Resources; Sex education.

Online resources

https://researchautism.org/self-advocates/sex-ed-for-self-advocates/

Includes information related to:

- Puberty
- Consent
- Relationships and dating
- Sexual orientation
- ASD specific

www.kidshealth.org

- Puberty
- Reproduction

www.plannedparenthood.org

- Includes information related to:
  - o Birth control
  - o Abortion
  - o Gender and sexual orientation
  - o Terminology
  - o ASD-specific information
  - o reproduction

Www.urbandictionary.com

- Current and common slang definitions

www.medlineplu.gov

- Puberty

Clinician's Guide to Sexuality and Autism
ISBN 978-0-323-95743-4
https://doi.org/10.1016/B978-0-323-95743-4.00022-9

- Menstruation

www.aboutkidshealth.ca

- Reproduction
- Puberty

www.npr.org

- Gender identity and terminology

www.genderspectrum.org

- gender identity

www.bpl.org

hotline for LGBTQA + related concerns

www.youthline.ca

- gender identity
- sexual orientation

www.pflag.org

- gender identity
- sexual orientation

Teaching social skills

The Autism Partnership Social Skills Group by **Justin B. Leaf, Ph.D., BCBA-D, Christine M. Milne, Ph.D., BCBA-D, Jeremy A. Leaf., M.A., BCBA, Jonathan M. Rafuse, M.S., BCBA, Joseph H. Cihon, Ph.D., BCBA-D, Julia L. Ferguson, M.S., BCBA, Misty L. Oppenheim-Leaf, M.A., BCBA, Ronald Leaf, Ph.D., John McEachin, Ph.D, Toby Mountjoy, M.A., BCBA**.

PEERS for Young Adults: Social Skills Training for Adults with Autism Spectrum Disorder and Other Social Challenges.

By Elizabeth Laugeson.

Crafting Connections ***Contemporary applied behavior analysis (ABA) for enriching the social lives of persons with Autism Spectrum Disorder*** by Mitchell Taubman, Ph.D., Ron Leaf, Ph.D., and John McEachin, Ph.D.

The Science of Making Friends: Helping Socially Challenged Teens and Young Adults by Elizabeth Laugeson.

Books about sex

Guide to getting it on by Paul Joannides.

The Book of Happy, Positive, and Confident Sex for Adults on the Autism Spectrum … and Beyond! By Michael John Carley.

Books about puberty

The Care and Keeping of You (Revised): The Body Book for Younger Girls by Valorie Schaefer and Josee Masse.

The Care and Keeping of You 2: The Body Book for Older Girls by Dr. Cara Natterson and Josee Masse.

The Girls Body Book (Fifth Edition): Everything Girls Need to Know for Growing Up! (Puberty Guide, Girl Body Changes, Health Education Book, Parenting Topics, Social Skills, Books for Growing Up) by Kelli Dunham RN, BSN.

The Boys Body Book (Fifth Edition): Everything You Need to Know for Growing Up! (Puberty Guide, Health Education, Books for Growing Up) by Kelli Dunham RN, BSN.

CHAPTER 22

Concluding thoughts

Abstract

This book has taken us through a number of topics relevant to sexuality and sexual safety for autistic individuals. The goal of this book was to openly discuss and outline the issues requiring our collective attention, with the hope that the sexual needs of autistic individuals can be more widely acknowledged and consistently supported.

Keywords: Autism; Sexual health; Sexual safety; Sexuality education; Sexuality.

This book has taken us through a number of topics relevant to sexuality and sexual safety for autistic individuals. The goal of this book was to openly discuss and outline the issues requiring our collective attention, with the hope that the sexual needs of autistic individuals can be more widely acknowledged and consistently supported.

The state of sexuality education is woeful, for those who are neurotypical, and even more alarmingly, for those with disabilities. The topic itself is controversial, which leads some families, teachers, and other caregivers to avoid the topics. The world is unforgiving, however, and a lack of information and education can have dire consequences. Autistic individuals are more likely than others to have negative sexual experiences, to be sexually abused, and to be exploited in other ways. It is essential that educators and caregivers provide them with the information, skills, and compassion they need to navigate their sexuality, claim their gender and sexual identities, and secure their sexual health.

We have reviewed a wide variety of instructional methods that are well-suited to delivering both content knowledge and social navigation skills. The effective instructional methods that have been used to teach many other skills are relevant in this context as well. It may be especially helpful to examine some of the procedures noted for their utility in teaching complex aspects of sexual health.

Including content in the areas associated with sexuality is part of a comprehensive curriculum, and is necessary. We have provided a curricular

Clinician's Guide to Sexuality and Autism
ISBN 978-0-323-95743-4
https://doi.org/10.1016/B978-0-323-95743-4.00019-9

outline to guide instruction in a number of areas. While some of the instructional areas are clear and noncontroversial, others are more complex. In many ways, the first part of the book covers the aspects of sexuality we are most comfortable with and which may already be included in education plans, but which may also still lack nuanced instruction. In the body parts progression, goals include understanding the language used to refer to body parts, both in a scientifically accurate manner and in typical slang terms used in their region/community. While the knowledge of the appropriate terms may be helpful in health and legal contexts (as in the case of an abuse investigation), it is also important to expose the individual to terms commonly used in informal social circumstances. Goals for menstrual care focus on hygiene and on independence. While both of these skills have been represented in curricular approaches, it is important to look at the components emphasized here, and how they are linked to independence and safety.

There is also a substantial focus on health, represented in the reproduction and birth control progression and in the health and hygiene skills. Indeed, the special knowledge and care of reproductive health is preventative, and can also help the individual to identify and report problems that should be assessed.

Much of the other content focuses on areas that are often underrepresented and ignored. The identification of goals in law and in online safety is related to the data on the increased vulnerability of autistic people to sexual violence and exploitation. The focus on sexual acts; on sexual abuse prevention and reporting; and on social skills helps to ensure that the individual learns about and understands sexual behavior and recognizes violations of behavioral norms in sexual contexts. This is extremely important, especially since an uninformed individual is both at risk for victimization and for being identified as a perpetrator. The understanding of laws governing sexual behavior and sexual content, and of what behaviors are acceptable and unacceptable, is vital and can prevent a host of problems.

The inclusion of material about instruction in masturbation, sexual orientation, and gender identity may be the content that readers found most difficult or challenging. Indeed, parents, teachers, and caregivers often struggle to discuss these topics with children and students who do not have disabilities. This is further complicated by society's lack of acknowledgment of autistic individuals as sexual beings. It is easy to ignore this dimension of their experience in the world, and there may not be much initiation of the topic from them. Furthermore, these are topics that are conversational lightning rods, often separating individuals based on strong opinions, deeply held beliefs, or religiously influenced practices. Nevertheless, it is clear that individuals with autism have sexual dimensions to their lives, sexual needs, and sexual preferences. It is also clear that autistic individuals tend to identify as nonbinary at a higher rate than neurotypical individuals. Helping the autistic individual to understand, navigate, and explore these essential parts of their identity is key to providing them with comprehensive care.

Appropriate intervention should always focus on choice making, preferences, and empowerment of the individual to determine every aspect of their life. In sexuality, this is perhaps even more salient and necessary. The curricular targets here are designed to ensure a broad sampling of the topics where choice and preference are relevant. Please note the emphasis on the dynamic nature of these preferences, as individuals are free to explore and change preferences throughout their lives.

It is our hope that this book will support autistic individuals' sexual knowledge and safety by providing a framework for instruction, and by helping caregivers to acknowledge the importance of recognizing autistic people as sexual beings. It is also our hope that this book may demystify some of the instruction needed, and provide targets for review, instruction, discussion, and exposure. We sincerely hope that this book can help destigmatize conversations around sexuality, sexual health, and personal safety, and provide sound instruction and compassionate support for autistic individuals in identifying their needs, preferences, and identities. We also sincerely hope that the use of this book helps to increase positive outcomes and reduce negative experiences in the lives of autistic people.

References

Addison, L. R., Piazza, C. C., Patel, M. R., Bachmeyer, M. H., Rivas, K. M., Milnes, S. M., & Oddo, J. (2012). A comparison of sensory integrative and behavioral therapies as treatment for pediatric feeding disorders. *Journal of Applied Behavior Analysis, 45*(3), 455–471. https://doi.org/10.1901/jaba.2012.45-455

Åker, T. H., & Johnson, M. S. (2020). Interviewing alleged victims with mild and moderate intellectual disabilities and autism: A field study of police-investigated cases of physical and sexual abuse in a Norwegian national sample. *Journal of Intellectual Disability Research, 64*, 782–792. https://doi.org/10.1111/jir.12771

Akers, J. S., Higbee, T. S., Gerencser, K. R., & Pellegrino, A. J. (2018). An evaluation of group activity schedules to promote social play in children with autism. *Journal of Applied Behavior Analysis, 51*(3), 553–570.

Alexander, N., & Gomez, M. T. (2017). Pleasure, sex, prohibition, intellectual disability, and dangerous ideas. *Reproductive Health Matters, 25*(50), 114–120. https://doi.org/10.1080/09688080.2017.1331690

APA Presidential Task Force on Evidence-Based Practice. (2006). Evidence-based practice in psychology. *American Psychologist, 61*, 271–285.

Backman, B., & Pilebro, C. (1999). Augmentative communication in dental treatment of a nine-year-old boy with Asperger syndrome. *ASDC Journal of Dentistry for Children, 66*, 419–420.

Barnard-Brak, L., Schmidt, M., Chesnut, S., Wei, T., & Richman, D. (2014). Predictors of access to sex education for children with intellectual disabilities in public schools. *Intellectual and Developmental Disabilities, 52*, 85–971.

Behavior Analyst Certification Board. (2020). *Ethics code for behavior analysts*. https://bacb.com/wp-content/ethics-code-for-behavior-analysts/

Bennett, K., Gutierrez, A., & Honsberger, T. (2013). A comparison of video prompting with and without voice-over narration on the clerical skills of adolescents with autism. *Research in Autism Spectrum Disorders, 7*, 1273–1281.

Bloor, D., Ballantyne, C., Gillespie-Smith, K., Wilson, C., & Hendry, G. (2022). Investigating the challenges of teaching sex education to autistic learners: A qualitative exploration of teachers' experiences. *Research in Developmental Disabilities, 131*.

Calabrò, R. S., Pioggia, G., Contrada, M., & Cerasa, A. (2022). Editorial: Sexual coach in high-functioning autism: A growing need. *Brain Sciences, 12*, 964. Retrieved from: https://doi.org/10.3390/brainsci12080964

Cazalis, F., Reyes, E., Leduc, S., & Gourion, D. (2022). Evidence that nine autistic women out of ten have been victims of sexual violence. *Frontiers in Behavioral Neuroscience*. https://doi.org/10.3389/fnbeh.2022.852203

Cengher, M., Budd, A., Farrell, N., & Fienup, D. M. (2018). A review of prompt-fading procedures: Implications for effective and efficient skill acquisition. *Journal of Developmental and Physical Disabilities, 30*(2), 155–173.

Chambless, D. L., & Ollendick, T. H. (2001). Empirically supported psychological interventions: Controversies and evidence. *Annual Review of Psychology, 52*(1), 685–716. https://doi.org/10.1146/annurev.psych.52.1.685

Chapman, L., & Trowbridge, M. (2000). Social stories for reducing fear in the outdoors. *Horizons, 11*(3), 39–40.

Charlop, M. H., Dennis, B., Carpenter, M. H., & Greenberg, A. L. (2010). Teaching socially expressive behaviors to children with autism through video modeling. *Education and Treatment of Children, 33*, 371–393.

Cicero, F. R. (2019). Shaping effective masturbation in persons with developmental disabilities: A review of the literature. *Sexuality and Disability, 37*, 91–108. https://doi.org/10.1007/s11195-018-9551-y

Cihak, D. F., Smith, C. C., Cornett, A., & Coleman, M. B. (2012). The use of video modeling with the picture exchange communication system to increase independent communicative initiations in preschoolers with autism and developmental delays. *Focus on Autism and Other Developmental Disabilities, 27*(1), 3–11.

Conallen, K., & Reed, P. (2016). A teaching procedure to help children with autistic spectrum disorder to label emotions. *Research in Autism Spectrum Disorders, 23*, 63–72.

Davies, A. W., Balter, S., van Rhijn, T., Spracklin, J., Maich, K., & Soud, R. (2021). Sexuality education for children and youth with autism spectrum disorder in Canada. *Intervention in School and Clinic*. https://doi.org/10.1177/10534512211051068. Advance online publication.

Dewinter, J., De Graaf, H., & Begeer, S. (2017). Sexual orientation, gender identity, and romantic relationships in adolescents and adults with autism spectrum disorder. *Journal of Autism and Developmental Disorders, 47*, 2927–2934. https://doi.org/10.1007/s10803-017-3199-9

Dogan, R. K., King, M. L., Fischetti, A. T., Lake, C. M., Matthews, T. L., & Warzak, W. J. (2017). Parent-implemented behavioral skills training of social skills. *Journal of Applied Behavior Analysis, 50*, 805–818.

Dotson, W. H., Leaf, J. B., Sheldon, J. B., & Sherman, J. A. (2010). Group teaching of conversational skills to adolescents on the autism spectrum. *Research in Autism Spectrum, 4*, 199–209.

Dowd, T., Czyz, J. D., O'Kane, S. E., & Elfson, A. (1994). *Effective skills for child-care workers: A training manual from boys town*. Boys Town, NE: Boys Town Press.

Esch, B. E., & Carr, J. E. (2004). Secretin as a treatment for autism: A review of the evidence. *Journal of Autism and Developmental Disorders, 34*(5), 543–556. https://doi.org/10.1007/s10803-004-2549-6

Fentress, G. M., & Lerman, D. C. (2012). A comparison of two prompting procedures for teaching basic skills to children with autism. *Research in Autism Spectrum Disorders, 6*(3), 1083–1090.

Ferguson, J. L., Milne, C. M., Cihon, J. H., Leaf, J. B., McEachin, J., & Leaf, R. (2021). Using the teaching interaction procedure to train practitioners to implement the Cool versus Not Cool™ procedure. *Behavioral Interventions, 36*, 211–227.

Francis, D. (2016). 'I felt confused; I felt uncomfortable... my hair stood on ends': Understanding how teachers negotiate comfort zones, learning edges and triggers in the teaching of sexuality education in South Africa. In *Global perspectives and key debates in sex and relationships education: Addressing issues of gender, sexuality, plurality and power* (pp. 130–145). London: Palgrave Pivot.

Garfinkle, A. N., & Schwartz, I. S. (2002). Peer imitation: Increasing social interactions in children with autism and other developmental disabilities in inclusive preschool classrooms. *Topics in Early Childhood Special Education, 22*(1), 26–38.

Garvey, N., & Senn, C. Y. (2014). Sexuality and sexual violence. In D. L Tolman, & L. M. Diamond (Eds.), *Chief), APA Handbook of Sexuality and psychology* (Vol. 1, pp. 339–382). American Psychological Association.

Gill, M. (2015). *Already doing it: Intellectual disability and sexual agency*. USA: University of Minnesota Press.

Graham, L. F., & Padilla, M. (2014). Sexual rights for marginalized populations. In D. L Tolman, & L. M. Diamond (Eds.), *Chief), APA Handbook of Sexuality and psychology* (Vol. 2, pp. 251–266). American Psychological Association.

Grosberg, D., & Charlop, M. (2014). Teaching persistence in social initiation bids to children with autism through a portable video modeling intervention (PVMI). *Journal of Developmental and Physical Disabilities, 26*(5), 527–541.

Hancock, G., Stokes, M. A., & Mesibov, G. (2020). Differences in romantic relationship experiences for individuals with an autism spectrum disorder. *Sexuality and Disability, 38*, 231–245. https://doi.org/10.1007/s11195-019-09573-8

Harriage, B., Blair, K. S. C., & Miltenberger, R. (2016). An evaluation of a parent implemented in situ pedestrian safety skills intervention for individuals with autism. *Journal of Autism and Developmental Disorders, 46*, 2017–2027.

Herrick, S. J., & Datti, P. A. (2022). Autism spectrum disorder and sexual minority identity: Sex education implications. *American Journal of Sexuality Education, 17*, 257–276. https://doi.org/10.1080/15546128.2021.2002225

Herson, L., Hart, K. A., Gordon, M. J., & Rintala, D. H. (1999). Identifying and overcoming barriers to providing sexuality information in the clinical setting. *Rehabilitation Nursing, 24*, 148–151. https://doi.org/10.1002/j.2048-7940.1999.tb02162.x

Horner, R. H., Carr, E. G., Halle, J., McGee, G., Odom, S., & Wolery, M. (2005). The use of single-subject research to identify evidence-based practice in special education. *Exceptional Children, 71*(2), 165–179.

Ingvarsson, E. T., & Hollobaugh, T. (2010). Acquisition of intraverbal behavior: Teaching children with autism to mand for answers to questions. *Journal of Applied Behavior Analysis, 43*(1), 1–17.

Jacobson, J. W., & Mulick, J. A. (1994). Facilitated communication: Better education through applied ideology. *Journal of Behavioral Education, 4*(1), 93–105. https://doi.org/10.1007/BF01560511

Jacobson, J. W., Mulick, J. A., Foxx, R. M., & Kryszak, E. (2015). History of fad, pseudoscientific, and dubious treatments in intellectual disabilities: From the 1800s to today. In *Controversial therapies for autism and intellectual disabilities* (pp. 65–90). Routledge.

Jacobson, J. W., Mulick, J. A., & Schwartz, A. A. (1995). A history of facilitated communication: Science, pseudoscience, and antiscience science working group on facilitated communication. *American Psychologist, 50*(9), 750.

Kassardjian, A., Taubman, M., Rudrud, E., Leaf, J. B., Edwards, A., McEachin, J., Leaf, R., & Schulze, K. (2013). Utilizing teaching interactions to facilitate social skills in the natural environment. *Education and Training in Autism and Developmental Disabilities, 48*, 245–257.

Kellaher, D. C. (2015). Sexual behavior and autism spectrum disorders: An update and discussion. *Current Psychiatry Reports, 17*, 25. https://doi.org/10.1007/s11920-015-0562-4

Kendall, N. (2014). Sexuality education. In D. L Tolman, & L. M. Diamond (Eds.), *Chief, APA Handbook of Sexuality and psychology* (Vol. 2, pp. 339–371). American Psychological Association.

Kodak, T., & Grow, L. L. (2011). Behavioral treatment of autism. *Handbook of applied behavior analysis*, 402–416.

Koegel, R. L., Bradshaw, J. L., Ashbaugh, K., & Koegel, L. K. (2014). Improving question-asking initiations in young children with autism using pivotal resposne treatment. *Journal of Autism and Developmental Disorders, 44*, 816–827.

Krantz, P. J., & McClannahan, L. E. (1993). Teaching children with autism to initiate to peers: Effects of a Script-fading procedure. *Journal of Applied Behavior Analysis, 26*, 121–132.

La Roche, M. J., & Christopher, M. S. (2009). Changing paradigms from empirically supported treatment to evidence-based practice: A cultural perspective. *Professional Psychology: Research and Practice, 40*, 396–402.

Leaf, J. B., Oppenheim-Leaf, M. L., Call, N. A., Sheldon, J. B., Sherman, J. A., Taubman, M., McEachin, J., Dayharash, J., & Leaf, R. (2012). Comparing the teaching interaction procedure to social stories for people with autism. *Journal of Applied Behavior Analysis, 45*, 281–298.

Leaf, J. B., Taubman, M., Bloomfield, S., Palos-Rafuse, L., Leaf, R., McEachin, J., & Oppenheim, M. L. (2010). Increasing social skills and pro-social behavior for three children diagnosed with autism through the use of a teaching package. *Research in Autism Spectrum Disorders, 3*, 275–289.

Leaf, J. B., Taubman, M., Leaf, J., Dale, S., Tsuji, K., Kassardjian, A., Alcalay, A., Milne, C., Mitchell, E., Townley-Cochran, D., Leaf, R., & McEachin, J. (2015). Teaching social interaction skills using cool versus not cool. *Child and Family Behavior Therapy, 37*, 321–334.

LeBlanc, L. A., Coates, A. M., Daneshvar, S., Charlop-Christy, M. H., Morris, C., & Lancaster, B. M. (2003). Using video modeling and reinforcement to teach perspective-taking skills to children with autism. *Journal of Applied Behavior Analysis, 36*(2), 253–257.

Libby, M. E., Weiss, J. S., Bancroft, S., & Ahearn, W. H. (2008). A comparison of most-to-least and least-to-most prompting on the acquisition of solitary play skills. *Behavior analysis in practice, 1*(1), 37–43.

Longino, E., Richling, S. M., McDougale, C. B., & Palmier, J. (2022). The effects of mastery criteria on maintenance: A replication with most-to-least prompting. *Behavior Analysis in Practice, 15*(2), 397–405.

Lovaas, I. (1981). *The ME book*. Austin, TX: Pro-Ed.

Lovaas, O. I. (1987). Behavioral treatment and normal educational and intellectual functioning in young autistic children. *Journal of Consulting and Clinical Psychology, 55*(1), 3.

MacDonald, R., Clark, M., Garrigan, E., & Vangala, M. (2005). Using video modeling to teach pretend play to children with autism. *Behavioral Interventions: Theory and Practice in Residential and Community-Based Clinical Programs, 20*(4), 225–238.

MacDuff, G. S., Krantz, P. J., & McClannahan, L. E. (2001). *Prompts and prompt-fading strategies for people with autism*.

MacManus, C., MacDonald, R., & Ahearn, W. H. (2015). Teaching and generalizing pretend play in children with autism using video modeling and matrix training. *Behavioral Interventions, 30*(3), 191–218.

Mann, L. E., & Travers, J. C. (2020). A systematic review of interventions to address inappropriate masturbation for individuals with autism spectrum disorder or other developmental disabilities. *Review Journal of Autism and other Developmental Disorders, 7*, 205–218. https://doi.org/10.1007/s40489-019-00192-9

Matson, J. L., Adams, H. L., Williams, L. W., & Rieske, R. D. (2013). Why are there so many unsubstantiated treatments in autism? *Research in Autism Spectrum Disorders, 7*(3), 466–474. https://doi.org/10.1016/j.rasd.2012.11.006

McCoy, K., & Hermansen, E. (2007). Video modeling for individuals with autism: A review of model types and effects. *Education and Treatment of Children*, 183–213.

McDaniels, B., & Fleming, A. (2016). Sexuality education and intellectual disability: Time to address the challenge. *Sexuality and Disability, 34*, 215–225. https://doi.org/10.1007/s11195-016-9427-y

Miller, U. C., & Test, D. W. (1989). A comparison of constant time delay and most-to-least prompting in teaching laundry skills to students with moderate retardation. *Education and Training in Mental Retardation*, 363–370.

Milne, C., Leaf, J. A., Leaf, J. B., Cihon, J. H., Torress, N., Townley-Cochran, D., Taubman, M., Leaf, R., McEachin, J., & Oppenheim-Leaf, M. (2017). Teaching joint attention and peer to peer communication using the cool versus not cool procedure in a large group setting. *Journal of Developmental and Physical Disabilities, 29*, 777–796.

Miltenberger, R., Gross, A., Knudson, P., Bosch, A., Jostad, C., & Breitwieser, C. (2009). Evaluating behavioral skills training with and without simulated in situ training for teaching safety skill to children. *Education and Treatment of Children, 32*, 63–75.

Mostert, M. P. (2001). Facilitated communication since 1995: A review of published studies. *Journal of Autism and Developmental Disorders, 31*(3), 287–313.

Nikopoulos, C. K., & Keenan, M. (2004). Effects of video modeling on social initiations by children with autism. *Journal of Applied Behavior Analysis, 37*(1), 93–96.

Nuernberger, J. E., Ringdahl, J. E., Vargo, K. K., Crumpecker, A. C., & Gunnarsson, K. F. (2013). Using a behavioral skills training package to teach conversation skills to young adults with autism spectrum disorders. *Research in Autism Spectrum Disorders, 7*, 411–417.

Nuzzolo-Gomez, R., Leonard, M. A., Ortiz, E., Rivera, C. M., & Greer, R. D. (2002). Teaching children with autism to prefer books or toys over stereotypy or passivity. *Journal of Positive Behavior Interventions, 4*(2), 80–87.

Ohlsson Gotby, V., Lichtenstein, P., Långström, N., & Pettersson, E. (2018). Childhood neurodevelopmental disorders and risk of coercive sexual victimization in childhood and adolescence - a population-based prospective twin study. *Journal of Child Psychology and Psychiatry, 59*, 957–965. https://doi.org/10.1111/jcpp.12884

Palmen, A., Didden, R., & Arts, M. (2008). Improving question asking in high-functioning adolescents with autism spectrum disorders: Effectiveness of small-group training. *Autism, 12*(1), 83–98.

Parchomiuk, M. (2022). Sexuality of people with intellectual disabilities: A proposal to use the positive sexuality model. *Sexuality and Culture, 26*, 418–448. https://doi.org/10.1007/s12119-021-09893-y

Phillips, E. L., Phillips, E. A., Fixsen, D. L., & Wolf, M. M. (1971). Achievement place: Modification of the behaviors of pre-delinquent boys within a token economy. *Journal of Applied Behavior Analysis, 4*, 45–59.

Phillips, E. L., Phillips, E. A., Fixsen, D. L., & Wolf, M. M. (1974). *The teaching-family handbook* (2nd ed.). Lawrence, KS: University Press of Kansas.

Picard-Pageau, W., & Morales, E. (2022). Interventions on sexuality for adolescents with autism spectrum disorder: A systematic review. *Sexuality and Disability, 40*, 599–622. https://doi.org/10.1007/s11195-022-09737-z

Plavnick, J. B., Sam, A. M., Hume, K., & Odom, S. L. (2013). Effects of video-based group instruction for adolescents with autism spectrum disorder. *Exceptional Children, 80*(1), 67–83.

Reynhout, G., & Carter, M. (2006). Social Stories for children with disabilities. *Journal of Autism and Developmental Disorders, 36*(4), 445–469.

Rowe, C. (1999). Do social stories benefit children with autism in mainstream primary schools? *Special Education: Forward Trends, 26*(1), 12–14.

Sala, Hooley, Attwood, A., Mesibov, G., & Stokes. (2019). Autism and intellectual disability: A systematic review of sexuality and relationship education. *Sexuality and Disability, 37*, 353–382. https://doi.org/10.1007/s11195-019-09577-4

Sarokoff, R. A., & Sturmey, P. (2004). The effects of behavioral skills training on staff implementation of discrete-trial teaching. *Journal of Applied Behavior Analysis, 37*(4), 535–538.

Schneider, M., & Hirsch, J. S. (2020). Comprehensive sexuality education as a primary prevention strategy for sexual violence perpetration. *Trauma, Violence, & Abuse, 21*, 439–455. https://doi.org/10.1177/1524838018772855

Schumaker, J. B., Pederson, C. S., Hazel, J. S., & Meyen, E. L. (1983). Social skills curricula for mildly handicapped adolescents: A review. *Focus on Exceptional Children, 16*(4).

Shillingsburg, M. A., Bowen, C. N., & Shapiro, S. K. (2014). Increasing social approach and decreasing social avoidance in children with autism spectrum disorder during discrete trial training. *Research in Autism Spectrum Disorders, 8*(11), 1443–1453.

Smith, T. (2001). Discrete trial training in the treatment of autism. *Focus on Autism and Other Developmental Disabilities, 16*(2), 86–92.
Solomon, D., Pantalone, D. W., & Faja, S. (2019). Autism and adult sex education: A literature review using the information-motivation-behavioral skills framework. *Sexuality and Disability, 37*, 339–351. https://doi.org/10.1007/s11195-019-09591-6
Stanojević, Č., Neimeyer, T., & Piatt, J. (2021). The complexities of sexual health among adolescents living with autism spectrum disorder. *Sexuality and Disability, 39*, 345–356. https://doi.org/10.1007/s11195-020-09651-2 (2021).
Stevenson, J. L., Harp, B., & Gernsbacher, M. A. (2011). Infantilizing autism. *Disability Studies Quarterly, 31*, 1–14. https://doi.org/10.18061/dsq.v31i3.1675
Test, D. W., Richter, S., Knight, V., & Spooner, F. (2011). A comprehensive review and meta-analysis of the social stories literature. *Focus on Autism and Other Developmental Disabilities, 26*(1), 49–62.
Tolman, D. L. (2006). Through a lens of embodiment: New research from the center on gender and sexuality. *Sexuality Research and Social Policy, 3*, 1–7. https://doi.org/10.1525/srsp.2006.3.4.1
Travers, J., & Tincani, M. (2010). Sexuality education for individuals with autism spectrum disorders: Critical issues and decision making guidelines. *Education and Training in Autism and Developmental Disabilities*, 284–293.
Walker, G. (2008). Constant and progressive time delay procedures for teaching children with autism: A literature review. *Journal of Autism and Developmental Disorders, 38*(2), 261–275.
Waugh, R. E., Alberto, P. A., & Fredrick, L. D. (2011). *Simultaneous prompting: An instructional strategy for skill acquisition. Education and Training in Autism and Developmental Disabilities* (pp. 528–543).
Weiss, M. J. (2001). Expanding ABA intervention in intensive programs for children with autism: The inclusion of natural environment training and fluency based instruction. *Behavior Analyst Today, 2*, 182–187.
Wolfberg, P. J., & Schuler, A. L. (1993). Integrated play groups: A model for promoting the social and cognitive dimensions of play in children with autism. *Journal of Autism and Developmental Disorders, 23*(3), 467–489.
World Health Organization. (2006). *The world health report 2006 Working together for health.* World Health Organization. https://apps.who.int/iris/handle/10665/43432

Further reading

Aljehany, M. S., & Bennett, K. D. (2020). A comparison of video prompting to least-to-most prompting among children with autism and intellectual disability. *Journal of Autism and Developmental Disorders, 50*(5), 1714–1724.
DiGennaro Reed, F. D., Novak, M. D., Henley, A. J., Brand, D., & McDonald, M. E. (2017). Evidence-based interventions. In *Handbook of social skills and autism spectrum disorder* (pp. 139–153). Cham: Springer.
Gerhardt, P. F., Cauchi, J., & Gravino, A. (2022). Sexuality and sexuality education with individuals with autism: What you should know but probably don't. In *Handbook of quality of life for individuals with autism spectrum disorder* (pp. 417–429). Cham: Springer.
Grow, L. L., Carr, J. E., Kodak, T. M., Jostad, C. M., & Kisamore, A. N. (2011). A comparsion of methods for teaching receptive labeling to children with autism spectrum disorders. *Journal of Applied Behavior Analysis, 44*, 475–498.
Gruskin, S., Yadav, V., Castellanos-Usigli, A., Khizanishvili, G., & Kismödi, E. (2019). Sexual health, sexual rights and sexual pleasure: Meaningfully engaging the perfect triangle. *Sex and Reproductive Health Matters, 27*, 29–40. https://doi.org/10.1080/26410397.2019.1593787

Gutierrez, A., Jr., Bennett, K. D., McDowell, L. S., Cramer, E. D., & Crocco, C. (2016). Comparison of video prompting with and without voice-over narration: A replication with young children with autism. *Behavioral Interventions, 31*(4), 377–389.

Leaf, J. B., Leaf, J. A., Alcalay, A., Kassardjian, A., Tsuji, K., Dale, S., ... Leaf, R. (2016). Comparison of most-to-least prompting to flexible prompt fading for children with autism spectrum disorder. *Exceptionality, 24*(2), 109–122.

Leaf, J. B., Leaf, R., McEachin, J., Taubman, M., Ala'i-Rosales, S., Ross, R. K., ... Weiss, M. J. (2016). Applied behavior analysis is a science and, therefore, progressive. *Journal of Autism and Developmental Disorders, 46*(2), 720–731.

Leaf, J. A., Leaf, J. B., Milne, C., Townley-Cochran, Oppenheim-Leaf, M. L., Cihon, J. H., Taubman, M., McEachin, J., & Leaf, R. (2016). The effects of the cool versus not cool procedure to teach social game play to individuals diagnosed with autism spectrum disorder. *Behavior Analysis in Practice, 9*, 34–49.

Leaf, J. B., Mitchell, E., Townley-Cochran, D., McEachin, J., Taubman, M., & Leaf, R. (2016). Comparing social stories™ to cool versus not cool. *Education and Treatment of Children, 39*, 173–186.

Mogavero, M. C. (2016). Autism, sexual offending, and the criminal justice system. *Journal of Intellectual Disabilities and Offending Behaviour, 7*, 116–126. https://doi.org/10.1108/JIDOB-02-2016-0004

Reed, F. D. D., Reed, D. D., Baez, C. N., & Maguire, H. (2011). A parametric analysis of errors of commission during discrete-trial training. *Journal of Applied Behavior Analysis, 44*(3), 611–615.

Schmidt, E. K., Brown, C., & Darragh, A. (2020). Scoping review of sexual health education interventions for adolescents and young adults with intellectual or developmental disabilities. *Sexuality and Disability, 38*(3), 439–453.

Sex Ed state Law and policy chart: SIECUS state profiles.(2021). https://siecus.org/wp-content/uploads/2021/12/2021-Sex-Ed-State-Law-and-Policy-Chart-3.pdf

Index